SUPER SEARCHERS on WALL STREET

TOP INVESTMENT PROFESSIONALS
Share Their Online Research Secrets

Amelia Kassel
Edited by Reva Basch

CyberAge Books

Information Today, Inc.
Medford, New Jersey

First Printing, 2000

Super Searchers on Wall Street:
Top Investment Professionals Share Their Online Research Secrets
Copyright © 2000 by Amelia Kassel

Super Searchers, Volume III
A series edited by Reva Basch

Library of Congress Cataloging-in-Publication Data

Kassel, Amelia.
    Super searchers on Wall Street : top investment professionals share their online research secrets / Amelia Kassel ; edited by Reva Basch.
        p. cm. – (Super searchers ; v. 3)
    Includes bibliographical references and index.
    ISBN 0-910965-42-0
        1. Investments—Computer network resources. 2. Investments—Information services. 3. Internet (Computer network) I. Basch, Reva. II. Title. III. Series.

    HG4515.95 .K37 2000
    025.06'3326—dc21

                                                                00-039658

Printed and bound in the United States of America

Publisher: Thomas H. Hogan, Sr.
Editor-in-Chief: John B. Bryans
Managing Editor: Janet M. Spavlik
Copy Editor: Dorothy Pike
Production Manager: M. Heide Dengler
Cover Designer: Jacqueline Walter
Book Designer: Jeremy M. Pellegrin
Indexer: Sharon Hughes

Dedication

I dedicate this book to Richard, who once called me the rock in his garden, but who is also a pillar of strength, my own private chef, and the joy of my life. And to my children and grandchildren—Mark, Laura, Russ, Christopher, and Nicholas. Nor would this dedication be complete without a tribute to three wonderful and influential people in my life—my mother, my father, and my sister Lucy.

About The Super Searchers Web Page

At the Information Today Web site, you will find *The Super Searchers Web Page*, featuring links to sites mentioned in this book. We will periodically update the page, removing dead links and adding additional sites that may be useful to readers.

The Super Searchers Web Page is being made available as a bonus to readers of *Super Searchers on Wall Street* and other books in the Super Searchers series. To access the page, an Internet connection and Web browser are required. Go to:

www.infotoday.com/supersearchers

Table of Contents

Foreword

Seven years ago, the first Super Searchers book started unlocking the secrets of professional information detectives. But today, everyday investors and professional financial analysts use a rich array of search engines, online data services, and investment Web sites, packed with charts, graphs, news, background, and analysis. In this new world of lay information experts, why would someone want to invest in distinguishing themselves as a Super Searcher on Wall Street? One might even ask, "Who needs Super Searchers?"

People who know the value of Super Searchers will scoff at those questions and enjoy the know-how that Amelia Kassel has gathered in *Super Searchers on Wall Street*. Those who wonder if Super Searchers are necessary might take a hint from the growing population of corporate concierge services, personal shoppers, and grocery delivery vans, or from the continued albeit changing role of travel agents, or even doctors and lawyers. In a world where it seems that any piece of information is available to a ten-year-old with a search engine, what are people paying for when they hire a lawyer, a personal shopper, or a corporate concierge? People are paying for time—now more than ever—or for better results than they could get themselves, or to be able to turn their own talents to their own jobs.

People on Wall Street are no different. They are looking for what they can't get from search engines:

- A search engine doesn't know the end user's business, its goals and strategies, its markets, customers, and competitive threats, or its language, concepts, and rumors.

- A search engine, even with the best relevancy ranking algorithms, doesn't know what's important and not important to each individual user.

- A search engine doesn't know how a user wants information packaged, what to highlight, or what to leave out.

- A search engine, even with the best language and domain experts behind its indexing scheme, is slow to respond to emerging trends.

- Any single search engine, even one with the ability to cross-search multiple databases, only covers a finite set of sources.

For all these things, Wall Street needs Super Searchers. And, judging by the accounts Amelia Kassel has gathered in this book, Super Searchers are being well utilized on Wall Street.

Readers of *Super Searchers on Wall Street* will visit with ten information and investment professionals and find what really distinguishes a Super Searcher from even the best search engine. Among other offerings, they will find:

- An insightful explanation of the stock analyst's job—and where to go on the Web for a more detailed profile

- How to exploit information sources for risk, fraud, and litigation analysis, for private placements and mezzanine structures, for real estate investment trusts, and for company valuation

- How the Series 7 exam can help a researcher

- Why everything worth searching for is found in pieces, and how to deliver structured data from multiple sources

- Who repackages free Web content and why investment professionals will pay for it

- How to cross-check data against multiple sources

- What data and functions a user may be overlooking in premier desktop services like Bloomberg

- A rich analysis of the ability of the Internet to support industrial-strength investing—and where to go for what's missing

- What is *not* online, what a searcher needs to know about what is still on paper, on CD-ROMs, or in specialized libraries, and when a telephone is still the best tool

Amelia Kassel's presentation benefits both new and experienced investment professionals, as well as personal investors who need to save time, get better results, or turn their attention more quickly to other priorities.

The obvious "secret" in this book is that a Super Searcher blends equal parts of passion, talent, and knowledge. Readers with a passion for information or for investing will value this book as a source of knowledge to develop their talent.

Nancy James
Director, Investment Information Services
Fidelity Management Research & Co.

Acknowledgments

I'd like to thank the 10 talented and special people I interviewed for participating and for the exceptionally hard work they contributed. I would also like to extend my deepest thanks to my editor, Reva Basch, for thinking up the Super Searchers book series and for her understanding and always considerate and gentle responses to me with incisive and important editorial changes. John Bryans, Editor-in-Chief of CyberAge Books, has also played a key role, always patient, supportive, and upbeat. Without the perseverance of all these wonderful people, and others who supported them, I would never have been able to go forth.

I would also like to acknowledge those who have influenced my career as an independent information professional: the late and truly great Sue Rugge, the phenomenally brilliant Barbara Quint, and Roger Summit, founder of Dialog Information Services, without whom I could not have gone online when I did. Absent these unique individuals, my career of the past fifteen years would not have been launched. To all of those whom I have met along the way who have encouraged and influenced me, I wish to extend my sincerest thanks, too.

Introduction

Before millions of users came to know about the World Wide Web, Reva Basch's book, *Secrets of the Super Net Searchers,* explored every aspect of making effective use of the Internet. The searchers Reva interviewed showered readers with substantial, precise, and inspiring instructions about how they, too, could mine the wealth of information that had suddenly exploded onto the world scene. The Super Searchers revealed their research techniques and procedures, the scope and capabilities of the online systems and search tools they used, and the drawbacks and advantages of both Internet-based and proprietary online services and sources. They also shared their own personal hints, tips, maneuvers, and manipulations for effective online research. Readers learned about the hot search engines of the day and about resources like gopher, Archie, and VERONICA—then-new, but now passé, Internet research tools.

At that point in 1996—eons ago in Internet time—the Super Net Searchers had already embarked on their voyage through cyberspace with an almost intuitive understanding of the magnitude of its soon-to-be ubiquitous presence. Since then, the World Wide Web has emerged, advanced, and established itself as a major societal trend. Most of the early Internet utilities and jargon are now history, having been replaced by a host of newer technologies, software, and concepts. The Internet has come to play a major role in millions of people's lives.

The World Wide Web is now more casually known as "the Web." A host of new search engines has materialized and continues to evolve, adding new services while fine-tuning existing features. Next-generation search engines come down the pike on a regular basis, building on their predecessors' strengths and competing to acquire favor with consumers.

Newer search technologies encompass concept searching, pattern matching or "fuzzy" searching, and natural language queries. Concept searching allows for intelligent assumptions about the search terms a user has entered. Pattern or "fuzzy" searching compensates for misspellings and spelling variations, which the traditional Boolean search engines do not. Natural language queries make it possible to enter search requests using the same plain-English syntax that we use when speaking. This is important because many users are not trained in advanced search techniques and don't have the time or interest to learn them.

Of course, we know that these au courant technologies can still lead to inconsistent or irrelevant results. Often, we must do more work before we have what we really need. Nevertheless, the increasing improvements in search engine functionality and ease of use are gradually giving users a semblance of an organized approach to finding information on the Web.

The early characterization of the Internet as the world's largest library with all the books scattered on the floor is changing. Search engines, intelligent agents or "searchbots," metasearch engines, subject-specific metasites, and the current wave of vertical portals for particular topics and industries—each new development has added dimensions and capabilities that make searching the Internet easier, faster, and more productive.

There is little question that everyone online today is witness to a revolution in technology that will forever change our lives. As the blitzy, glitzy electronic uprising continues, innovative companies, content, services, systems, and features impart distinctive change. Every day, Web entrepreneurs invent new businesses and business models, and new software and resources for users of online information.

Simultaneously with the development of the Internet, significant socioeconomic trends have affected the financial services industry and millions of individual investors. Such trends are reflected in this new collection of Super Searcher interviews, *Super Searchers on Wall Street*. Investment activity has increased extraordinarily during the past several years. Individual investors, endeavoring to take control of their financial futures, are emerging as a savvy breed of newcomers to the investment world. Their expertise is bolstered by an explosion of financial information in books, newsletters, television programs, newspaper articles and columns, and by the power of the Internet. All this has leveled the playing field. Individual investors and small companies and businesses can now get critical decision-making information that only large corporations and institutional investors were privy to heretofore.

In the past, you might have visited your local public library for help in making investment decisions. Investment research was a time-consuming process, but some of the larger libraries, at least, could afford the expensive investment-related periodicals, newsletters, and directories. The phrase "knowledge is power" is absolutely relevant to the world of investing. And now, especially because of the Internet, investors have all kinds of information at their fingertips: instant, real-time stock quotations; up-to-the-minute news stories on critical events affecting a company's financial situation; and investment analysts' reports with buy, hold, or sell recommendations. The Internet provides a profusion of choices regarding specialized online investment sources, sites, software, and tools. Just about everything an investor needs for understanding market and industry trends, and companies they want to invest in, is now available online.

Investors are now online in droves and executing their own stock trades, using more than one hundred fifty online trading companies. One of these, Muriel Siebert & Co. (SiebertNet) [202, see Appendix A], was named number one discount broker in the 1999 annual survey by *SmartMoney* magazine, a joint venture between the Hearst Corporation and Dow Jones & Company, Inc. Some firms have become household names because of consistent television advertising; Charles Schwab, E*TRADE, and Ameritrade come to mind. Traditional stock brokerage firms such as Merrill Lynch, seeing the business opportunity presented by the growing electronic marketplace, have entered the online trading fray.

Here are some statistics and facts:

- The number of online trading accounts grew to almost 9.7 million in June 1999 from 3.7 million in 1997. [Source: *Daily News* (New York), November 23, 1999, Pg. 37]

- By 2003, more than 20 million people in the United States will trade online, a four-fold increase from today. [Source: *Evening Standard* (London), February 15, 2000, Pg. 41]

- The growth rate on the Internet for online trading was 53 percent between 1998 and 1999. [Source: Distribution Management Briefing, September 15, 1999, from a study by Cybercitizen Finance, a division of the online market research firm Cyber Dialogue]

- Research conducted by Jupiter Communications found that the online brokerage market will grow more than the financial services sector and increase its asset pool to over 3 trillion dollars by 2003. The report also forecast that 41 percent of U.S. households with stocks will possess online trading accounts in 2003. [Source: *Internet Business News*, October 1, 1999]

- Online trading volume spurted 55 percent in the fourth quarter of 1999, according to an analysis by Piper Jaffray, and about 16 percent of Wall Street's daily trades are now done through computer-based accounts. [Source: *Internet Business News*, October 1, 1999]

- The mutual-fund industry controls more than $6 trillion in equity, bond, and money-market funds. [Source: *Business Week*, January 24, 2000, Pg. 66]

- The average American now uses 15 banking and investment "products"—checking, credit cards, mortgage, mutual funds, life insurance, and so on—from five different companies. [Source: *Money*, December 1999, Pg. 134]

• About 18 percent of U.S. individual investors say they traded stocks, bonds, or other securities through the Internet in 1999, up from 10 percent the previous year. Almost half those users plan to trade over the Internet more often in coming months. [Source: *Seattle Post-Intelligencer*, November 5, 1999, Pg. B7, from the Securities Industry Association's Fifth Annual Investor Survey]

The growth of the investment industry is reflected in the popularity of investment-related media programming. For many years, *Wall $treet Week* with Louis Rukeyser has been one of the leading television programs focused on the world of finance. Although not an investor herself, my mother has watched this program religiously every Friday since the seventies, when it first began. Viewers think highly of Mr. Rukeyser, an urbane and affable man with an intelligent presence and presentation about the sometimes-unfamiliar subject of stocks and bonds.

As a supplement to *Wall $treet Week*, an investor today can turn on cable television at almost any hour and find a financial news or investment advisory discussion. Time-wise, the daytime financial programs compete with the soaps and the infamous TV talk shows. CNBC provides all-day coverage of the stock market with discussions of new IPOs, Internet stocks, and the economy, and interviews with movers and shakers who offer investment advice to their cable/financial devotees. URLs are given out freely throughout the day so viewers can follow up when they want more in-depth information by signing on to the Internet.

The average investing consumer is aware of the need for information to help understand what's going on. However, investors—especially new investors—must be careful: Internet message boards and chat rooms are known for postings that promote certain companies in order to make their stocks soar. The media has covered numerous investment-related online scams. For those dazzled by the get-rich-quick scenarios that some online trading firms portray in their ads, a recent study indicated that online traders generally underperform those who trade by phone and use the more traditional approach, a middleman stockbroker or financial advisory service. Reasons given for failure include cost of commissions, especially when trading frequently; taxes; and—a less tangible cause—a loss of discipline that may lead to unwise trading practices.

Nevertheless, investors are encouraged by the growth in the investment industry itself and by the relatively long-term good economy that has kept inflation rates low. More consumers have money to invest and are gravitating toward mutual funds and annuities in record numbers. The potential size of the investing community has grown, too. The baby-boom generation, 77 million strong, began turning 50 in 1996. Many are saving for retirement and have started to build personal fortunes through investing. They are beginning to reap the benefits of their parents' hard work and careful savings practices. As a group, boomers are taking many more investment risks than their parents, who were constrained by Depression-era economics after the 1929 Wall Street crash. Many boomers have become affluent. They must embark on an investment education as they find themselves with extra funds and with retirement on the horizon. The more informed they are, the better their investment decisions will be.

The generation behind them, known as Generation X, is another large demographic group, some 40 million strong. Many Gen-Xers have become active in the stock market, and some are very serious investors. The American Stock Exchange surveyed 500 25- to 35-year-olds with annual incomes of more than $30,000 per year and found that:

> • Eighty-eight percent believe they won't be able to count on Social Security as a source of income when they retire. As a result, many are extremely interested in saving for the future. One young investor described how he spends three hours a day researching companies to invest in. [Source: Knight-Ridder Tribune Business News: *Sun-Sentinel* (South Florida), November 1, 1998]

• Seventy-nine percent already are investing for long-term goals, such as retirement, major purchases, or "just for the thrill of it."

• Fifty-two percent of Gen-Xers have already invested in mutual funds, compared to 25 percent of the general public.

• Thirty-two percent own individual stocks and 24 percent own bonds, compared to 20 percent of the general public.

• This generation has started making contributions to 401(k)s or other deferred compensation plans, and is much more money-minded than were boomers at that age. [Source: *PR Newswire*, November 7, 1996, "Brokerage Industry Off to Strong Start with Young Clients"; "While Only 33% Have Brokerage Accounts, 92% Are Satisfied with Service"; "Firm's Good Name Is #1 Factor in Choosing Broker"; and Yerton, Stewart, *New Orleans Times-Picayune*, February 23, 1997, P. F4. The Factor; Generation X Investors Urged to Exploit the Benefits of Youth]

One study suggests that online traders are growing from the influx of Generation-Xers who are flocking to such services. [Source: *Web Finance*, July 19, 1999, "Study of Affluent Investors by J.D. Power & Associates"]. Moreover, Generation-X mutual fund shareholders are saving money at a faster rate than older investors, according to the Investment Company Institute's 1998 Profile of Mutual Fund Shareholders. They are also more likely to participate in defined contribution plans, are better educated, and are more computer literate, according to the data. ICI's profile indicates that 22 percent of all mutual fund shareholders are Generation-Xers, 51 percent are Baby Boomers aged 34 to 52 years, and 27 percent are of the so-called Silent Generation, aged 53 years or older. The average total of mutual fund assets held by households led by Generation-X investors is $22,700, the ICI data showed. For Baby Boomers, it is $63,800 and, for the Silent Generation, $147,600. One headline even suggests that "Generation X may be financially smarter than its elders" and cites a study by

Scudder Kemper Investments. "Those belonging to Generation X—people between 22 and 33 years old—are more work-oriented and more willing to take responsibility for their financial future than their elders." This study found that 71 percent of Generation-Xers are saving a portion of their weekly income at a rate similar to older generations. Scudder Kemper researchers found that the saving habits of Generation-Xers have been influenced by their lack of faith in Social Security—only 10 percent expect to get full benefits. [Source: *Associated Press State & Local Wire*, July 18, 1999]. Finally, a survey by the Lincoln Financial Group found that almost two thirds—64 percent—of adults aged 18 to 34 years are already saving for retirement. A total of 44 percent of people in that age bracket are starting to save for retirement before they reach the age of 25 years, and 18 percent of Gen-Xers are starting before they hit the age of 20 years. The study also looked at 401(k) plan participants who put aside a larger portion of their savings (60 percent), although their total amount saved per month was the same as most Americans, about $300. [Source: *Pensions and Investments*, May 3, 1999, Pg. 8]

To briefly summarize major macrotrends of the past five to ten years, we've seen economic stability, increasing wealth, enormous growth in investment activity fueled by changing demographics and new technology, and unfathomable amounts of information accessible through multiple mass-media outlets. Guidance in identifying and using this information is crucial—for selecting the right information and for preventing information overload. Even experienced investors who already know how to accomplish their financial goals must continue to gain a deeper understanding, and to refine their techniques in the face of changing economic, social, and technological conditions.

Super Searchers on Wall Street is set against this backdrop of our times. In this book, I interview 10 top investment researchers who work for companies that offer financial, economic, legal, and strategic advice on complex business and investment issues. They work with and for financial industry professionals such as investment analysts, financial advisors, attorneys, and high-level specialists in investment banking, corporate finance, mergers and acquisitions, and due diligence.

They provide penetrating insights, a multitude of valuable online resources, and a significant collection of tips and techniques for researching companies and industries. This book takes you inside some of the largest investment companies in the world and brings you into contact with niche institutional investment advisory firms and other companies that provide various services to Wall Street.

The results of my interviews, I believe, are striking. In this book, the Wall Street Super Searchers, collectively, have created a body of knowledge that can be applied to both personal investing and developing or enhancing a career in financial industry research. The Wall Street Super Searchers demonstrate how they find data crucial to the detailed financial analyses that underlie professional investment recommendations and deal-making. They share their knowledge of information sources used by investment banks, financial advisory services, mutual fund companies, federal regulators, and deal-makers. They disclose the most important and useful resources available on commercial online database services, the Internet, and CD-ROM. They discuss their reasons for using traditional databases and which ones in particular they consider authoritative, current, and trustworthy.

They also share their favorite Web sites for investment research and explain how and why they use the Internet for obtaining electronic information that they can't readily get elsewhere. Several of the Super Searchers suggest that the Internet, although still in its infancy, is undoubtedly the technology for serving up financial information in the future. These experts stress the importance of learning about and keeping up to date on the newest technologies and databases.

Let me introduce you to the Super Searchers on Wall Street and highlight particular specialties. In this book, you'll get to know:

- Hodi Poorsoltan, Founder and Information Manager of the Information Center at General Motors Investment Management Corp. Hodi uses an extremely wide range of online services to provide background and investment information to his users.

- Gary Klein, an individual investor and Management and Economics Librarian at Hatfield Library, Willamette University, in Salem, Oregon. He has been investing since childhood. Gary offers some of his own personal investment philosophy.

- Tish Williams, at the time of her interview, was Senior Editor and a columnist for *Upside,* a business technology magazine for executives, senior-level technology managers, and investors. Tish was also the *Upside* Webmaster and used the Web daily for research. She reveals some of her favorite sites.

- Janet Hartmann, Research Librarian and Registered Securities Representative at William Blair & Co., a Midwestern investment bank. Janet provides an arsenal of crucial information used by financial analysts.

- Richard Harrison, Researcher and Partner in Global Securities Information, Inc., the producer of LIVEDGAR, a value-added online database service for Securities and Exchange Commission filings.

- Robert J. Magri, Principal in and Market Data Vendor Manager for State Street Global Advisors, one of the largest investment management firms in the world. Bob has vast knowledge of financial data and online technology. He describes online resources used for financial market data and analytical tools used by institutional investors for investment decisions.

- Roberta Grant, Business Librarian and Investigative Analyst for Kroll Associates, Canada, which serves the security interests of major corporations, investment banks, and stock exchanges. Robby reveals how she uncovers fraudulent activities by conducting due diligence and background checks for stock exchanges, corporations, investment banks, and individual investors.

- Chris Carabell, Senior Vice President and Investment Manager Researcher at Liberty Asset Management Company.

Chris selects investment managers for mutual fund products and uses an array of sources to monitor institutional manager portfolios.

• Martha DiVittorio, at the time of this interview, was Information Services Manager for Oliver Wyman & Company, a management consulting firm specializing in the financial services industry. Martha proactively solicited requests as a way to promote information services in her company.

• Nathan Rosen, Corporate Law Librarian for Credit Suisse First Boston, one of the world's largest global investment banking firms. Nathan describes his responses to complex business, investment research, and due diligence questions.

Some of the Super Searchers' titles and activities may seem a little unfamiliar at this point. By the time you finish this book, however, you will not only understand what they do, you will also have gained solid knowledge about online resources in the investment industry and how to use them yourself.

In the following paragraphs, I've summarized some of the important themes that came to light during the interviews.

Electronic Databases

Although I'm a veteran online searcher, I must admit that I hadn't heard of some of the online services and databases that the Wall Street Super Searchers use and had only a cursory knowledge of others. Some of the commercial online services described here, for example, are FactSet Data Services [71], Compustat [43], Datastream [50], Bloomberg [19], Lipper Analytical Services[133], Securities Data Corp. [199], CDB-Infotek [33], CourtLink [47], CaseStream [139], PACER [173], ADP [1], and Haver Analytics [94]. The Super Searchers use specialty CD-ROMs as well, including those for identifying institutional investment managers and their portfolios, and descriptions of venture capital and buyout firms. Wall Street Super Searchers also use the traditional online services well known to information professionals in other fields, such as Dialog [52], Lexis-Nexis [127], and Dow Jones Interactive [56]. In the interviews, they talk about how and why they use each of these different systems.

Terminology, Concepts, and Jargon

The financial services industry speaks a language of its own. Both individual investors and researchers working in financial institutions must have an understanding of the terminology and concepts that the industry uses. One Super Searcher explains that most of the employees at her company voluntarily become Registered Securities Representatives, which requires that they study for and pass a National Association of Securities Dealer (NASD) test. The preparatory materials are particularly helpful for learning and understanding financial terminology and regulations. Since the Wall Street Super Searchers used and emphasized many unfamiliar words, I have compiled an extensive glossary in Appendix B. Appendix B also includes a list of Web-based glossaries and dictionaries.

Value-Added Services

Wall Street Super Searchers not only conduct online research, but also provide value-added services by filtering and supplying just the information their users require. Some also prepare reports and recommendations. They emphasize that good writing, communication skills and a basic knowledge of spreadsheet software are essential to their jobs.

Trends

Here are some of the major trends garnered from interviewing the Wall Street Super Searchers:

- The Internet has leveled the playing field for individual investors who like to manage their own portfolios. Some sources are on the Web for free or at low cost. Online trading companies provide clients with research, too. The Super Searchers suggest a number of useful Web sites for background information and stock portfolio development.

• With the advent of the Web, thousands of financial industry professionals have access to information tools on their desktops. End users can now meet their basic, everyday information needs with online services such as Dow Jones Interactive and Bloomberg. The Wall Street Super Searchers, however, are busier than ever. They do not feel threatened by end-user searching, because they are involved with the more in-depth research required by these same users, who also demand value-added analysis or presentation. End users still contact professional researchers with the more complex and demanding research questions.

• During the past several years, we have seen a considerable number of library closures and layoffs throughout the business world. It's interesting to note, however, that two of the ten Wall Street Super Searchers were hired solely for the purpose of founding and creating a library. One interviewee currently operates without an in-house library, but discusses the value of centralizing information services within his company. He thinks a library would serve this need, and that one may be developed in the future. Another has seen her department grow in size, with an increased ratio of librarians to consultants on the staff. The overall trend is toward an increasing number of libraries, librarians, and information managers. All of this bodes well for information professionals. The financial services industry is knowledge intensive and requires more information and more information professionals, rather than fewer.

• The Super Searchers are proactive about serving their clients. They seek out opportunities for increasing services that go far beyond what many traditional librarians were trained, initially, to do.

- Wall Street Super Searchers gain experience in the use of many online services and do not limit themselves to just one or two favorites. They use whatever is necessary to get the job done.

Keeping Current

The Wall Street Super Searchers agree that keeping current isn't easy. They describe a great number and variety of sources—electronic, print, and in-person—for staying on top of financial and information industry developments. They all say that keeping current is crucial for maintaining an edge in their profession. The periodicals they read, the electronic discussion groups in which they participate, and the conferences and trade shows they attend provide an excellent guide for readers who want to stay on top.

Conclusion

As you read each Wall Street Super Searcher interview, you'll be exposed to many electronic systems, sources, and vendors. Their descriptions of typical research questions and projects illustrate how the Super Searchers apply their knowledge of online research tools and techniques. They serve, dynamically, a wide range of requests; they leap far beyond traditional roles. They are at the same time generalists and specialists, analysts and communicators. I'm convinced that their revelations will be directly applicable and useful to you. Every one of the Wall Street Super Searchers is on the cutting edge of the financial information scene and the technology required to find what's needed in just about any circumstance. We're fortunate that they were willing to share their knowledge and wisdom. I thank each and every one for the contribution he or she has made to this undertaking, which I am now pleased to share with you.

Hodi Poorsoltan
Information Center Manager

Hodi Poorsoltan is the Information Manager for General Motors Investment Management Corp., where he founded and operates the information center. He has extensive experience as an information specialist for major U.S. multinational investment banking and investment management corporations.

hodi.poorsoltan@gm.com

Tell me about your background and how and when you started working with investment-related research.

I have an undergraduate degree in history from the University of Georgia. I received my M.L.S. in 1980 from Pratt Institute Graduate School of Library and Information Science, in Brooklyn, New York. I had never dreamed of or planned on becoming a librarian. My initial interest and desire was to pursue graduate studies in history, cultural geography, or philosophy. But family and financial circumstances forced me toward a practical and reasonable solution, and I became a professional librarian quickly, in 14 months.

My first professional job was as a cataloger at the Brooklyn Public Library. It was a welcome relief to land a professional position during the tough job market of that period. I decided to become a corporate librarian because of my people-oriented and outgoing nature, a wish for more professional challenge, and better financial rewards. My first corporate job was at J. Walter Thomson, the advertising agency. I was hired as both a cataloger and researcher and stayed a year. My first truly corporate experience

15

came next, when I went to work for Peat Marwick Mitchell (now KMPG), where I acquired a sound business and finance background and research experience.

I became part of the investment banking world when I took a research position at Morgan Stanley's headquarters in New York City. I spent four years with Morgan Stanley in New York and another four years in their Tokyo branch office. While in New York, I was a researcher with four assistants. We were dedicated to mergers and acquisitions, corporate finance, and the real estate department. The nature of investment banking combined with the personal traits of our users—some were very difficult and arrogant individuals—created a potent and demanding work environment with endless rush requests.

In Tokyo, I managed a library of seven full-time and two part-time staff members. It was one of the greatest professional and life experiences to manage the largest non-Japanese corporate library in Tokyo while enjoying living, learning, and traveling in the Asia-Pacific countries. The Tokyo staff was highly dedicated, knowledgeable, and hard-working, and handled a very large number of requests from some 800 Tokyo staff members as well as several offices throughout the Asia-Pacific region.

You now work for General Motors Investment Management Corp. How would you describe your company in a nutshell?

General Motors Investment Management Corp. (GMIMCo) is the financial arm of General Motors in New York City. Our business is investment management, which is called "buy side," as opposed to investment banking, which is called "sell side." Our business is focused on long-term investment with the hope of best returns for the GM staff pension money. The nature of our business makes the work environment less demanding and more subdued than my investment banking experience at Morgan Stanley.

However, because of the ever-changing and highly competitive global business climate, GMIMCo has started to offer fund and money management services to outside parties, which will completely change the nature of our business. I can see that, soon, we will have a touch of greater intensity, as in my former job climate at Morgan Stanley. It seems that the ghost of investment banking is following me.

What kinds of online research did you conduct at Morgan Stanley?

I did detailed and general research on companies, products, industries, economics, markets, and SEC [196, see Appendix A] documents such as 10-Ks, 10-Qs, prospectuses, and others. We provided information services to the Morgan Stanley offices worldwide using various CD-ROM products and online systems such as Lexis-Nexis [127], Dialog [52], Dow Jones [56], Investext [121], CDA/Spectrum [32], Dun & Bradstreet [58], and Disclosure's [176] Compact D (now owned by Primark). In Tokyo, we also used Japanese-based systems like Nikkei [166] and Teikoku [212], which offered text and financial information on Japanese companies and on Japan as a whole in Japanese as well as English.

Since I've been with General Motors Investment Management Corp., Web-based searching has changed the nature of searching tremendously. Several information vendors now offer their services on the Web, sometimes as the only mode of delivery. End users—such as portfolio managers, for example—now have access to many of these sources on their desktops. These technological changes and innovations have transformed online and investment research considerably.

What's your work like now and what are your job responsibilities at GMIMCo?

I was hired to create the General Motors Investment Management Corp. Information Center from scratch in September of 1995. When I joined GMIMCo, there was no centralized information/research center. Although we're 100% part of

GM, our operation at GMIMCo is independent and separate from the General Motors operations worldwide. Our total staff in New York at GMIMCo, plus our Treasurer's Office (a separate GM entity), comes to nearly 300 members. I proposed and marketed information services to the Treasurer's Office with the approval of the GMIMCo managing director because I thought that it made good business sense. If the Treasurer's Office utilized the invested technology to its full extent, there was a greater possibility for financially securing the information center and my position as well.

At the start of my challenging task of building and promoting the information center, there was much uncertainty, spotty support, and slowness in getting people to use it. That's changed considerably. The Information Center now has a reputation as the place to get fast, accurate, and complete investment-related data. During the first six months of 1999, I've already done four times the amount of work I did during the entire year in 1996. At the beginning, I had two assistants to help me get started in organizing the Information Center. At present, I have one or, occasionally, two temps. I handle all the research inquiries for all our business units and departments such as Fixed Income, Equities, Real Estate, Asset Allocation, and International Investment.

I spend approximately 70 percent of my time on electronic online research. To keep track of work, I count units. Clients often ask a question that could have many components. For example, someone may want information on France; this could require researching the French economy, finding out about specific French companies, and learning rules and regulations. I consider each question separately, which gives me a more accurate count of usage of the Information Center by our various departments.

I average 400 to 500 or so units per month. I don't time myself. Some questions require a lot of time, like finding papers or research from organizations such as the Association for Investment Management and Research [13], the World Bank [238], the International Monetary Fund [114], or the United Nations [217]. It may take two to four hours to locate a working paper from any of these or from a university. But I still consider this type of question as one unit or one question.

What online database services do you use?

I use many online systems including Lexis-Nexis, Dialog, Dow-Jones, and First Call [79] Notes, which is real time and consists of one to four pages of news on public companies from major investment houses. They cover spin-offs, reorganizations, and any other news that affects a stock. I also use First Call Research Direct, which has research reports from one to more than 200 pages about companies, industries, products, and countries from various investment houses worldwide. Both First Call products are from Thomson Financial [215].

Another Web service from Thomson's Investext is Intelliscope [111]. It has analysts' reports similar to First Call Research Direct, but with a five- to six-week time lag. I use it primarily because some of the contributing companies are different than those in First Call. Other systems that I find useful are Standard & Poor's Market Insight [138], which is Web-based, with information on companies, countries, and industries. Market Insight includes financial data, text, analyses, and commentary and incorporates Standard & Poor's Stock Reports and Industry Surveys, DRI Economics [57], and Compustat financials [43]. A service that is valuable, particularly for SEC documents, is Disclosure's Global Access [53]. I also use ProQuest [179], which is Web-only and from Bell and Howell, which acquired UMI. It's great for trade and academic articles and papers not available from Lexis-Nexis and has graphics for articles that are only in text on Dialog.

For financial information, Datastream [50], a Primark product, offers thousands of historical data sets on inflation, interest rates, markets, stock exchanges, companies, and countries. I find that Dun & Bradstreet, via Lexis-Nexis, is the best place to go for private company reports, and it has global coverage. Bloomberg [19], a vast real-time system, offers detailed historical and up-to-the-minute information about stocks, industry trends, companies, countries, economies, real estate, markets, and political and general-interest news. I also use Compact D from Disclosure for historical and detailed financial, business, and product information on some 12,000 public companies. It's a CD-ROM and is updated monthly.

Many of GMIMCo's business units now have desktop access to some of these Web-based systems and sources, but I continue to assist them both in retrieving data and in playing the role of information consultant, advising them on how to tap the best sources for what they need. I have a small but useful print collection of investment-management-focused resources, but I do rely very heavily on electronic sources.

The number of online services you've mentioned is very impressive. Since you use so many different vendors, how do you know which system to use to answer a question?

It comes from many years of hands-on experience and keeping up-to-date. You really have to know all the systems very well, as well as what they cover. Any researcher will reach the stage of knowing the best source for a particular question over, say, two to three years, and will be able to choose the right system and sources for any given inquiry.

If I search the Current News Library in Lexis-Nexis and plan on also conducting the same search in Dow Jones Interactive, I can expect some overlap. In that type of situation, I exercise my judgment to avoid duplication. It's important not to overload and burden the users with too much or redundant information.

Apart from that, what to use depends on the nature of the inquiries. If a user wants historical, statistical data, I go to Datastream. For full articles from *The Wall Street Journal* or *Barron's*, I search Dow Jones Interactive because that's the only service with complete full text for both of those sources. In the case of industry- or product-related questions, I go to First Call Research Direct or Standard & Poor's Market Insight. For the bulk of general news and information, I go to one of the most comprehensive and up-to-date systems—and my favorite—Lexis-Nexis.

I think the same way about SEC-related questions. Many services now carry SEC filings. If the user is looking for a segment of a 10-K—such as a list of foreign subsidiaries, or real estate properties owned by a company—by using the right EDGAR system, I can pull just those parts required. I get most of my SEC reports from FreeEDGAR [84], which allows you to view the structural outline of an SEC filing first, and then hyperlinks to the section you want. This can be preferable to printing and scanning a whole 10-K, which may be hundreds of pages in length.

What types of research questions do you respond to?

Most of my research covers economic issues, theories, and market trends, such as the European Monetary Union, value at risk, political situations and development, risk management, emerging market countries, electronic commerce, and Asian and Latin American trade matters. I also search on historical data such as exchange rates between two currencies, inflation, and unemployment worldwide. I provide quick company information, detailed and extensive background on consumer and high-tech products or real estate issues, and biographical data on individuals as well.

I might be asked to identify some 97 companies in a particular industry group and review financial information about them. Then I'll use the Nexis Eclipse service, an electronic clipping system, to automatically retrieve new information on these companies on a daily, weekly, or monthly basis. With Nexis Eclipse, you can save several searches, each with a given name or title for easy recognition and recall as it fits your requirements, for a short or much longer period of time. There are situations in which I need to continue searching about the same companies for several months. First Call Research Direct offers tracking and saving searches under your own name or portfolio as well. You can also save your search criteria on Datastream and Bloomberg.

I'll monitor risk factors such as social, political, or economic issues that may concern our investments in various countries. For this, I use the Economist Intelligence Unit's (EIU) Country Reports [61] and *Euromoney* [67], both on Lexis-Nexis. EIU has detailed and very up-to-date country reports divided by segment, such as political climate or trade. I use ProQuest's Digital Dissertations to find Ph.D. theses related to economic issues and theories. These can be purchased by credit card and downloaded in PDF and read using the Adobe Acrobat Reader. Institutional subscribers have access to the entire database and others can have free "guest" access privileges that allow you to search citations and abstracts for all titles published this year and last.

Tell me about your use of the Internet.

I access Dialog, Dow Jones Interactive, Intelliscope, Market Insight, Global Access, FreeEDGAR, and ProQuest through the Web. In some cases, the Web is the only mode of delivery. Recently, our hardcopy monthly subscription to *Asian Venture Capital Journal*, a Hong Kong-based publication, changed from paper format to Web-based delivery in PDF. I have been using Amazon.com and Borders.com to purchase most of the library's business and finance books. It's generally less expensive and quite fast to order books online. I often pull various pieces of information such as derivatives, market reports, and press releases from several major investment houses' Web sites such as Morgan Stanley Dean Witter [148], Goldman Sachs [91], Merrill Lynch [145], and Donaldson Lufkin & Jenrette [55]. These sites provide general public information, but, since we are clients of all major sell-side investment houses, we are provided special client passwords that entitle us to a much more extensive list of reports and releases. When I add some of the professional and academic Web sites, I may be spending 65 percent of my research time on the Web.

Many of the Web sites you have described are subscription-based. What about your use of free or low-cost Web sites?

For financial news and information, I use MSNBC [151] or CNNfn, the CNN Financial Network [37]. I also use major search engines such as WebCrawler [231], Yahoo! [240], Lycos [135], Excite [69], and Infoseek [108]. I do find that search engine indexing and coverage has improved from the early days, but I still have more trust in the reliability, up-to-date coverage, and superior indexing of commercial databases.

University Web sites give me access to economic, business, and finance working papers that are very valuable and in demand by our economists at GMIMCo. I use many of the university sites to find case studies and working papers on economic theories and issues. For example, Harvard University Business School [93] and the University of Pennsylvania's Wharton School [233] provide many business- and finance-related publications, although most must be purchased with credit cards. Some of the association and organization Web sites are also terrific. You can download and print 70-to-80-page reports instantly in PDF from the World Bank or the United Nations, for example.

How do you prepare results for delivery to your users?

Part of it has to do with selecting just the information that's needed. I screen the right information from a system such as the Economist Intelligence Unit for, say, India or Turkey or other emerging-market countries. I may only need the economic section, or items in citation instead of full-text format. I pull and deliver exactly what's asked for. In the case of an industry analyst's report about the electronics industry from a firm such as Goldman Sachs, I'll also gather just the precise information rather than the whole report and deliver just what's needed.

What software programs do you use for post-processing your results?

I use Microsoft Word and Excel, and a version of Bloomberg called Open Bloomberg, which is a cross between Excel and Bloomberg. You open it as a spreadsheet before you do your search. Like Datastream, you can start a search in Excel—for instance, to create tables for 25 years of exchange rates between the Japanese yen and American dollar or for data from stock exchanges that can be turned into a graph. I open Excel first, before I execute the online search from Datastream, and the data is automatically downloaded into Excel.

How has Internet research affected your costs overall?

The arrival of the Internet as a means of information delivery has been driving prices down in a few products. Because of the stiff competition that vendors now face, things are changing. The new and upcoming Web-based companies such as LIVEDGAR [134] and FreeEDGAR offer free and low-cost access to SEC filings, and their products are similar to the traditional, expensively priced Disclosure Compact D and Global Access. The same is true in the case of Web-based Multex [153], a company that offers investment analysts' research reports on products, companies, and industries from hundreds of investment houses for less than the cost of First Call Research Direct.

Let's talk about how you stay current.

I receive regular email from the Special Libraries Association (SLA) [206] about various industry events. I also attend the annual SLA conference and the National Online Meeting [156], which is held every May in New York City. I receive updates and announcements in email and in print from Dialog, LIVEDGAR, Dow Jones, Disclosure, Datastream, *The Economist* [60], and Standard & Poor's. I receive product announcements and information from almost every information vendor in the U.S. as well. To expose myself to international and non-U.S. seminars and conferences, I attended the European Business Information Conference [68] in Dublin, Ireland, in 1999 and in Lisbon, Portugal, in 1998. I read several professional publications like *Information Outlook* from SLA, *ONLINE* [172], *EContent* [62] and *Information Today* [106]. I am also in regular contact with many information-related vendors and systems who give onsite demonstrations at my office of new products or enhancements to existing ones.

What has been your greatest success in your investment research experience?

The best success story in my four years here has to do with my providing answers to skeptical users and earning respect and credibility among the business units with which I work. Despite the fact that my users are a Web- and desktop-educated, computer-literate crowd, I fill in the missing pieces of information that they cannot locate or can't locate as fast as I can. When uncovering a piece of information becomes difficult for them, they turn to me. It has not always been all that easy working with young M.B.A.s who, at times, can be cocky and difficult. I think that being accepted as a professional in a corporation such as this is a challenge to many of my colleagues in the information industry.

What are some global or macro trends that have changed your research environment?

All professions, globally and across the board, are facing constant challenges from fast-changing technology. While dentists, telephone companies, airlines, grocery chains, and manufacturers all face tremendous change, the challenge is more acute in the case of the librarian and information specialist since it attacks and upstages the very core of our work, which is information. Most educated and computer-literate people can access and use at least some level of information directly without the help of an information professional. The corporate information specialist must now offer value-added services to meet the challenge.

Super Searcher Power Tips and Wisdom

➤ To keep track of work, I count units. Clients often ask a question that could have many components. I consider each question separately, which gives me a more accurate count of usage of the Information Center.

➤ Despite end-user desktop access, information specialists now play the important role of information consultant by advising their users about how to tap the best sources to meet selected requirements.

➤ Major investment houses provide free public information in addition to specialized reports and releases for buy-side subscribers.

Gary Klein
Individual Investor and Business Librarian

Gary Klein is Management and Economics Librarian at Willamette University's Hatfield Library in Salem, Oregon. He has been investing since childhood and uses his experience, education, and investment knowledge for both personal and professional gain.

gklein@willamette.edu
http://members.aol.com/tethered

Tell me about your background and how you became involved in investment research.

It goes back to childhood. My parents always had stock in two or three companies, and every year they sold one stock and bought one stock. Altogether, they typically had about one half-year's gross pay invested. They never had more than 20 or 30 shares. For me, it opened the door to not being allergic to stock market investments. As compared to other kids in the neighborhood, I felt that stocks were not something from outer space—buying stock was not strange or scary, nor was there ever a feeling of being on a roller coaster. My father made some money on his stocks, a bit more than if he had placed the money in the bank, and didn't lose anything. So, as a child, I felt comfortable about the concept of investing.

I started reading *Business Week* [25, see Appendix A] at the library around the age of twelve or thirteen, and gradually, as my reading level increased, I added *Fortune* [83] and other business sources. By the time I was in college, I was reading and thumbing through *The Wall Street Journal* [226], Moody's [146], and

Standard & Poor's [207] to learn more about how various companies were doing. I first put money into the stock market while I was a sophomore in college, when I realized that banks paid a better rate of return to their shareholders than they paid to their depositors. I bought four shares of stock in a regional banking firm for about $135, including commissions. At the time, I was attending a state university, majoring in computer science with the dream and goal of working for a bank to help find ways to eliminate paperwork and build profits. I thumbed through back issues of banking journals from 1925 forward. There was a good collection at the State University of New York (SUNY) at Buffalo, and I read such classics as the *Federal Reserve Bulletin*, which has tons of details about bank merger applications approved and denied by the Federal Reserve Board [74]. I also ran through several decades of trade magazines for commercial banks, savings banks, and savings and loan associations at SUNY's library.

I also started reading the business section of *The New York Times* [163] and would not miss a single issue, catching up even after I was out of town for winter break. I found out that the main office of the Buffalo and Erie County Public Library carried actual copies of 10-Ks, 8-Ks, 10-Qs, and proxy statements for hundreds of firms traded on the New York Stock Exchange [162]. They also had many Buffalo-area companies that were traded over the counter (OTC). I started attending shareholder meetings of local companies and soon found that I knew more about some of these firms than many of their directors, just by reading publicly available documents.

By the time I was working full-time at a bank in Buffalo, I had already attended more than ten shareholder meetings in Buffalo and Rochester, and was asked to be a "correspondent" for the Gilbert Brothers. Lewis D. Gilbert and John J. Gilbert of New York City had been shareholder activists for about 40 years when I first heard of them. They inherited a large stock portfolio when their parents died. While overseeing their stock portfolio, they often attended more than a hundred annual meetings of shareholders in a calendar year. As one of their correspondents, I attended shareholder meetings on their behalf, carrying their proxy cards for companies in the Western New York area from my home in Buffalo, New York. They used the process of submitting resolutions to corporations for shareholders to vote on as a means of initiating reform of corporate governance procedures. The motto of their nonprofit foundation was "dividends and democracy."

Over the years, I added a few shares of stock here and there, in banks, utilities, or local firms. The most I bought was 10 shares at a time, always in companies where the stocks traded at less than $30 per share. In my third year of full-time work at a Buffalo-based savings bank, I earned a profit-sharing payout of almost $1,000 in cash, in addition to my deferred earnings. I bought 22 stocks in one day, all with one share as a starter. This was in the days of Merrill Lynch's Sharebuilder Program that allowed you to get shares, down to four decimal places of a fraction, for a minimum fee of $1 and 4.5 percent commission over the purchase price. The manager of the Merrill Lynch office in Buffalo threatened to throw me out the door, but every one of the stockbrokers loved me, even though they nicknamed me "Mr. One Share."

By this time, I was on a first-name basis with all the business reporters at both of Buffalo's daily newspapers. Each had a full staff of three to eight people covering just the business beat. I started subscribing to *Barron's* [18] at home around 1983 and gradually added more companies to my portfolio, using dividend reinvestment plans to directly invest in firms beyond that initial one share per firm. By the time I left my career at a savings bank in January 1987, I owned shares in 140 different publicly traded firms with a portfolio of $64,000 and an average of nine shares per company. I stopped adding funds to that portfolio and began liquidating it while I was attending graduate school for my M.L.S.

While I was in graduate school, the Certificate of Deposit (CD) in my old retirement account came up for renewal. Since my former employer, a savings bank where I kept my IRA, was about to be shut down by the FDIC [72], I rolled my IRA certificates over to a stock brokerage IRA, buying shares in three companies. I later liquidated my "regular/cash" stock account, which was my nest egg, for the down payment on a home. I was working as a Business Librarian in Toledo, Ohio, at the time. I had taken that job right out of school in September 1988 and was there until 1995.

At the same time, my retirement stock portfolio was expanding nicely, just from reinvesting dividends into additional companies every now and then. After not being able to add to my retirement stock account, I received a windfall payment from my former employer's pension plan—a check for $22,000, which could be rolled into the stock IRA without much paperwork. I bought round lots in three pharmaceutical firms, using up ninety-nine percent of the pension payout.

Since that pension rollover in 1992, I have not added a single penny of cash into my stock retirement account other than the dividends I earned from those stocks. I've bought and sold stocks, usually buying only a hundred shares. I try to hold a stock forever. My trading philosophy is that if I can earn more than a 20 percent return on my investment in a single year, I don't hesitate to sell a stock. I have sold a number of stocks for 20 to 30 percent profit in just four to six months. I also have stocks that are now trading at half my purchase price. I try to invest for the long term. If someone is offering an obscene profit after a short holding period, however, I will not complain as I cash in my chips and use the proceeds to invest in a different company or industry.

As of 1999, I have 60 companies in that stock retirement account, with a market value equal to about four times my current gross salary. The shares in my regular, taxable cash account have held rather constant, about equal to my annual salary. I have tapped into those dividend streams many times, once selling a stock to give money to my parents when they were in dire financial shape. In the '80s, I used to spend hours each week poring over tons of financial information. I no longer try to read 500-plus annual reports or 200-plus 10-Ks each year, in addition to those from my own investments.

That's an historical overview of how I gradually became a stock market investor. I hope this gives you some idea about where I'm coming from in terms of my being both a business librarian and a self-made investor and researcher.

Why did you decide to become a librarian after such intense interest in the banking industry?

After working for 12 years at one bank, I went to library school at the State University of New York at Buffalo. One of the reasons I went to library school was that the bank I worked for was soon to be shut down by the FDIC, as were large numbers of banks during that time. At the bank, I primarily did research and development and market research, which included responsibilities like site location analysis and customer surveys for potential new products or alternate service charge schemes. I also did bank merger and divestiture analysis and other work, such as demographic studies to match people and products. I was involved with some internal operation activities, such as rerouting the courier system to make it more efficient between the branches. Also, I did some back-office work, such as random surveys of where our customers were distributed, which accounts had service charges waived, and average balances based on criteria, such as payroll deposit or social security.

At various times, I did regulatory analysis and prepared speeches for our president. The president was trying to lobby the local congressman who happened to be on the Banking Committee. We did lots of lobbying from 1980 to 1982, and this required analysis, which we could do more cost-effectively than a law firm. Since I had a wide range of research skills, I initially thought I could transfer my knowledge to other banks or market research firms specializing in the banking industry. But there was a declining employment market in 1987 for bankers and marketers in the Western New York area, and I began to look at other ways to use my knowledge base. I thought that by becoming either a government or a business librarian, I could transfer the knowledge that I had gained during the 12 years in banking.

What type of services and research have you used for your own portfolio research?

I had no access to online information until around 1987 or 1988 when the CDs for Disclosure [176] first surfaced in two libraries in my area, the public library and the local university library. Once people started discovering it, there was a waiting line. Today, I read *Barron's* and browse through *The Wall Street Journal*, which is also part of my job. I use the daily news broadcasting features of Infobeat [102], a Web service that offers general news, sports, legal, finance, and weather. The finance section allows you to build a portfolio. You can get a daily report by email of the high, low, and closing prices and one or two other statistics you can choose. You also have a choice of daily news for your stocks. You can choose to receive an alert at the middle of the day or at the end of the day. There are other options, too. I take a general market wrap-up with a quick summary of the daily market that includes things such as what Greenspan said today (and how people held their breath a little), a few sentences on bonds and gold and the like. The alerts run about three to four screens as email.

All in all, I monitor my stocks and about 100 other firms that I have interest in. I use Yahoo! Finance [241] to glance at headline news pertinent to my stocks. This site gives the last five news items on each company that you key in, plus the current day's trading activity, all free and with faster turnaround time than other services. On a monthly basis, I log into the SEC's EDGAR [196] to see recent SEC filings for my portfolio firms. I subscribe to a push service from my stockbroker that alerts me when certain activity has taken place for my companies and of company press releases and available analysts' reports with major changes and analysis of their industries. I set certain thresholds about what I will use and only look at this push service for about half my stocks outside of the banking industry.

Otherwise, my mailbox would overflow in just one business day. You can be inundated if you are not careful.

How do the online stock brokerage accounts work?

You set up an account with a minimum amount of money for trading. Because of the volume of trading going on, response time can be quite slow. Yahoo! is faster because it doesn't register each user every time, whereas online stock brokerage companies do. The two companies I use—Charles Schwab [34] and Waterhouse Securities, Inc. [229]—go through security checks for each user, which can slow things down considerably. Waterhouse Securities is a discount brokerage with hundreds of offices nationwide. It's a division of Toronto Dominion Bank, with services quite comparable to that of Charles Schwab.

Do these companies provide you with research as well as facilitate online trading?

Yes, although each uses different research providers. They don't all use the same wire service, for example. That's part of the reason I have accounts with two companies. Sometimes one or the other is just too slow or doesn't have what I want. Sometimes, when trying to get online at eight o'clock at night, it can take as many as three attempts to get a complete connection through America Online (AOL) [7], my preferred provider. I wait a minute and use the other firm or try connecting through Netscape, but that means I don't have access to some of AOL's proprietary services, which I find useful. The typical routine is a busy signal, most likely, between eight and eleven p.m. There are always some little glitches on AOL, but I can usually get online in a minute.

What financial services do you use on AOL?

I use news and quote services on AOL, especially because both Waterhouse and Schwab have erratic response times. Stock broker companies use lots of security layers and encryption that are visibly slow and quirky on my 486 machine at home, which still runs on Windows 3.11. I use AOL for my primary investment research and figure that the $24 a month is worth it just for the investment data that I get from them.

What kinds of information do you glean from studying stock quotes?

I either want to track my current stocks or add companies within a specific industry to my portfolio, in which case I'm watching to see what's going on with particular stocks in an industry. I may have a target of perhaps five to eight companies and the prices might change day by day. If I have the cash, I want to know which is the best one of this core pool of companies that I've identified in a fuzzy kind of way. From an operational point of view, I'm comfortable with the types of products and services these five companies offer, but I only have money for one and must decide which one to buy.

I compare dividend ratios, earnings to dividends, price to earnings, and concentration of ownership in terms of which ones are more volatile or which are more predictable. This information helps me decide what to do next. I'm also watching for ways to include a stock that contains the letter of the alphabet I need. One of my strategies is to have at least one company starting with every letter of the alphabet, because this is one way to diversify. It's one form of the random dart theory. The concept is that a blind chimpanzee throwing a dart might actually have a better chance of making money than the trained executive who's only reading the so-called tea leaves provided by a company's official press releases.

The random dart theory was hypothesized well over 40 years ago. Louis Rukeyser jokes about it on his television program when he asks how so many professional money managers can have a preference for a mutual fund that's worse than the average they're trying to mimic. The basic concept is that, if you randomly diversify, you will have fewer losses than someone who puts all their eggs in one basket. Conversely, of course, if one company takes a giant explosion of growth and profits, you will lose out on that exploding growth because you are diversified. At any rate, the random dart theory is supposed to help minimize the volatility of the total portfolio.

Do you use the Motley Fool Web site?

I've looked at it once or twice, and I just can't believe all the back-fence banter. A recent issue of *The Wall Street Journal* had a minute-by-minute analysis of the postings to one list for one company's chitchat. The article revealed that the two primary people speaking were trading in the very stock they were talking about, and were encouraging others, in effect, to move the market so that the two loudmouths could profit.

Tell me more about your professional library career and how your experiences in the stock market help students with investment research questions.

Students often require case studies about companies and, because of my experience, I can tell which ones they are more likely to find. I can steer students in the right direction with their company research, too, because I know when and why you'll find more information on one type of company than another. I'm also very experienced in knowing the ins and outs of EDGAR from the Securities and Exchange Commission, and I can show students tricks that are not clearly presented or explained on the SEC help screens.

What are some tips and "secrets" of using the SEC site?

One important feature is that the SEC search engine can search on headers other than company by name, but they don't tell you about this or other hidden factors. It's true that you cannot search by industry, but you can search for companies whose physical address is in a certain city, on a certain street, or in a certain ZIP code. It's important to know, also, that the system uses stop words like "First" or "State" or "Corporation," which are very common words, especially for names of banks. Yet they don't list their stop words anywhere, and this can make finding a company quite difficult. If you're looking for the First Central State Corporation and doing a keyword search, the response is that nothing matches, but there is no explanation as to why. If you don't know about the stop words, you'll miss important information. In fact, most users think you can only search the site by company name. I own stock in First State Bank Corp. and check the filings about it from time to time. To get around the stop word problem, you search by city or street. Of course, I have to either remember the street address or the name of the city, or look it up, and I can never spell Albuquerque, which is where one of the companies in my portfolio is located.

What other EDGAR products do you use?

Apart from the SEC Web site, I use Disclosure on CD-ROM. It has 101 different ways to search for companies. You can look for ratios, number of employees, or a specific dollar amount from a balance sheet. It has a lot of power when you want to screen companies by many different types of criteria. It's not as current as some sources because it's updated monthly.

Do you use Dialog or other commercial online vendors for finding more current information?

We've stopped using Dialog [52] during the last year. For the amount of use we have here, with only 140 business graduate students and twelve faculty members, I can typically find answers in various CD-ROM or print sources that we carry in the library. Given the Dialog monthly minimums and having to learn the unique command structure, it's a lot of overhead that I can bypass.

We have an account with Lexis-Nexis Academic Universe [128], a subscription database service. It's a subset of the larger Lexis-Nexis system and gives us access to wire services and some 70 daily newspapers that are online with just a 24-hour turnaround. This is very helpful to students who need information with a local angle. Some of their projects involve event analysis, which is a way of analyzing how certain events impact stock prices. By taking a company name through the wire service or local newspaper portion of Academic Universe, a student can track events and even clock them to the second. They can tell when an article hit the wire service or newspaper and analyze how good news or bad news affects the price of a stock, the reaction time of competitors, or how analysts reset their earnings projections according to news events. Students who take courses that involve event analysis are planning to become investment analysts, and Academic Universe is very helpful to their research.

What other databases do you use for students? We've talked about Disclosure. Do you use others such as Morningstar or Value Line?

We have Value Line [223] in print, and the students definitely use it. The public library has more of a demand for Morningstar [149] than we do. We also have the full range of the Moody's manuals but in print only. When I saw the online version at the American Library Association (ALA) [6] Conference, they were having a lot of response time problems. The company changed hands and is now called FISonline [80].

How has the Internet changed your investment research style?

I spend much more time online, probably about five hours a week. For instance, in the last six months I've been online a half-hour every morning. Once a week, I do an in-depth reading of the news. I used to look at stock prices once a week in a newspaper.

Now, I could be online all day if I wanted to. This can happen both at work and at home. That's not necessarily good because you can become locked into your machine if you don't realize that there's a life out there.

Let's turn to quality and reliability with regard to the Web. You've talked about the fact that some systems or servers are slow. What are your thoughts on the quality of information?

Some of the underlying news services that Web sites such as CNN [37] use, or even *The Wall Street Journal*, have not carried a single news item for six months on some stocks I own. It's as if they never received a quarterly or year-end earnings press release. In one case, there was no information about a bank in the Boston suburbs with over a billion dollars of assets for six entire months. I could see the stock prices moving up and down, but I couldn't find any news, and hardly any stock analysts followed it. In a situation like this, you can't find out why a company suddenly spikes two to three dollars a share. You can't find news on AOL, Schwab, Waterhouse Securities, or Yahoo! Finance.

Do you think you would find better or more complete information on commercial sources like Lexis-Nexis or Dow Jones Interactive?

Some of the services I just mentioned carry Bloomberg [19], Reuters [188], AP [9] UPI, [220], Dow Jones [56], and *The New York Times*, and yet nothing is picked up, even though the earnings come through in little columns in the daily fine print of *The New York Times* or *The Wall Street Journal*. In one case I know about, there was a problem because of name confusion with regard to a ticker symbol. For example, on AOL, every time I look up Texas Regional Bank Shares with the ticker symbol, TRBS, I get the Tribune Company, a Chicago-based media company with the ticker symbol TRB. The system just won't pull the company I want. Some of the price quoting and news services have problems when you are looking at stocks with special classes of shares trading. A case in point is the J. M. Smucker Company, the jam and jelly folks, NYSE symbol, SJM, with both Class A and B stock. Another one is Alberto-Culver, hair and personal care products, whose NYSE symbol is ACV, with both common and Class B.

You must have to be very much aware of how a system is pulling up information, especially when it comes to ticker symbols and acronyms.

That's right. But this information is not necessarily easy to find out about. Another problem is that some of the online database providers do a worse job of information input than others. Moody's has had a problem with this since they first tried doing anything in CD-ROM.

I found grotesque errors of all kinds. My favorite error was very weird: They listed Chase Manhattan Bank as having its principal banking done by some dinky savings and loan in Virginia.

Any idea why these errors occur?

Lord knows. I told a Moody's rep about this at the ALA (American Library Association) Conference, and he said, "You're kidding"—just before the database locked up for two minutes while pulling up a sample record of his choosing. Moody's does not have a good track record for correcting errors. I've pointed some out, but the errors remain. Now that Moody's FISonline is a, separate company and not part of any other complex, I hope they become more quality control-oriented.

But Moody's isn't the only one. Some of the errors that I've pointed out to UMI (now owned by Bell & Howell) and IAC (Information Access Company, now owned by Gale Group) were still there two years later. When you have a database with five years of data for hundreds of thousands of corporations, and it includes full-text history and accounting information, it's easy to have some errors. But when some are so visibly cockeyed, and the salesperson says "yes, yes," and then when you ask for follow-up and don't get a response … well, it's important to mention these problems.

Has the Internet changed your pricing structure?

We've dropped some of the paid databases and closed our accounts. We used to have Dialog and EPIC from OCLC. The OCLC EPIC service was integrated into the OCLC FirstSearch [169] service in July 1999 and isn't available anymore. I'm always able to help without using these vendors because so much is available on CD-ROM, or through flat-rate subscriptions, or from the Internet. We don't need really expensive online services that charge per minute. When a student asks for a specific brand name, say a mutual fund from a Morningstar Report, I ask if I can get someone else's analysis that's comparable in terms of respect within the industry, and then find what fits the bill. Even an analysis from something like *Barron's* magazine may fulfill the request.

Any horror stories you can tell regarding online investment research?

I can tell you a story about a wire service that gave the wrong ticker symbol for a bank in Arkansas. There were several banks with similar names, such as Horizon Bank, Horizon Bankcorp, Horizon Bank Corp., and Horizon Banks, Inc. When I found out about the stock symbol mix-up, I contacted all the companies to tell them that the wrong information was on the press release, but there were no retractions for more than four weeks. In another case, the shares of a West Virginia company spiked 25 percent, but there was no news from West Virginia to explain why. In some cases, all three major wire services have carried the identical wrong ticker symbol of a company, and, of course, people will invest in the wrong stock. You can see it actually happening based on the trading activity. I've seen these sorts of things happen more than once.

How do you stay current, both professionally and with regard to your personal investing?

Unlike many of my colleagues, I have never worried about keeping track of everything. I just do what I can to keep somewhat up-to-date on news, trends, and software. When I worked in banking, it was very clear that some employees at my bank spent enormous amounts of energy trying to figure out what one specific bank was doing in response to anything new that we offered. In the long run, it was not a productive use of their time or of our bank's resources, nor was it a profitable route to take.

Rather than worry about competition, I try to keep an eye out without being obsessed by it. Don't get me wrong; I browse the issues of several trade and professional magazines, including *EContent, ONLINE, Library Journal, American Libraries, Journal of Academic Librarianship, Library Trends, Library Quarterly, Reference Services Review (RSR), Reference and User Services Quarterly (RQ), CRL News,* and *College and Research Libraries.* I have been an active participant in several library-oriented email lists like BUSLIB-L [26]. I also take advantage of the table-of-contents alerting service from CARL UnCover [30], with about 25 journals and magazines in my profile, along with weekly keyword searches on LIBRAR* and OREGON. I don't focus my energy on just one aspect of librarianship since I work for a liberal arts college and have to work with faculty in religion and philosophy, and with students in other departments, too, in addition to my primary responsibility for the departments of management and economics.

I have worked with colleagues at other libraries who were compulsive about having to read the daily news from certain newspapers or checking certain news services at specific times each day. I don't go that far, but I do try to browse through *The Wall Street Journal* each day. I also try to watch the nightly news as it can only be uniquely capsulized by *The Daily Show* on the Comedy Central cable channel. I am not kidding about this. I listen to an all-news radio station each workday morning. I don't try to read the local newspaper on a daily basis because of the inferior quality of our local rag. The business section is seldom more than one page of news on weekdays. But I do glance at the State Capitol column, letters to the editor, and regional news every Sunday and two to three times during the week.

How do you maintain an edge?

With regard to investing, with only very rare exceptions, I always buy stock in companies that I personally know about through my research. Online research, in particular, has become integral to this process for me. I have a T-shirt—I posted a picture of it on my Web site—that says, "In the defense of freedom and literacy, libraries are the most powerful weapons we have: Use them!" I find that using information, libraries, and online research definitely helps me maintain an edge.

What do you see as major global or industry trends that will affect electronic research, investment research, or the future for professional business researchers?

The growing number of push services, combined with the steady growth of news and business portals, is building toward information overload. It's clear that even librarians themselves want to find the Holy Grail—the answers to their questions online, on the Web, and free. They increasingly fail to consider looking at standard print sources that almost any regional public or academic library would have on the shelves.

I see this again and again in the questions posted to BUSLIB-L, a mailing list for business librarians. Librarians are being assaulted by so many different types of sources and ever-changing brand names and Web addresses that they're going bonkers. They're losing the ability to conduct a basic reference negotiation. It's a growing occurrence on BUSLIB-L for someone to ask for a 20-year time series of very specific data, saying, "I've talked to the publishers and looked at similar data from the United Nations, but I would rather find it all in one Web site, for free." Increasingly, they will not take "no" for an answer. They are wasting their time and the time of BUSLIB-L readers, trolling up and down the Internet, looking for someone else's freely available database, when they could have had access to the data from a book and have entered it manually into a spreadsheet a week ago.

I have even seen librarians from esteemed M.B.A. schools ask for electronic-only sources, eschewing the standard print sources that they've already paid for and that are perfect for the data they are asking to see. I've also worked in for-profit companies filled with impatient executives who expect librarians to be superhuman and get everything in a snap, in the precise spreadsheet format that the executive envisions. Increasingly, librarians are responding by asking, "How high do you want me to jump?", rather than being pragmatic and negotiating the requests.

My suggestion is to speak up and ask people to clarify or restate what they are asking for. Think of it as "reference negotiation." Ask your requestors to tell you what they are trying to locate. If what they are looking for does not exist, what would they like as a substitute? Ask what they are going to do with the information. Ask what they would do if that particular piece or format of information does not already exist. Work with them; ask them to explain to you, up-front, their rationale.

All this will help you find accurate, reliable sources for answers. Explain that you want to be able to both support their hypotheses and understand the circumstances in which their hypotheses might fail. Be prepared to work together; they will gain a better understanding of the data structures while you will gain a better understanding of what they are striving for. As one last thought and piece of advice, try to make sure to mix some humor into your relationships before you hit the road looking for wacky things when bosses snap their fingers.

Super Searcher Power Tips and Wisdom

➤   The SEC EDGAR search engine can be searched by more than just company name. Companies can be searched by street address, city, or ZIP code.

➤   By taking a company name through a wire service or local newspaper, you can track events and even clock them to the second. You can analyze how good news or bad news affects the price of a stock, the reaction time of competitors, or how analysts reset their earnings projections according to news events.

➤   With only very rare exceptions, I always buy stock in companies that I personally know about through reading and research about the company and its products and services.

➤   Increasingly, librarians are responding by asking, "How high do you want me to jump?", rather than being pragmatic and negotiating the requests. My suggestion is to speak up and ask people to clarify or restate what they are asking for. Think of it as "reference negotiation."

Tish Williams
Investment Magazine Editor and Columnist

Senior Editor and columnist for *Upside* magazine at the time of this interview, Tish Williams is now a columnist for TheStreet.com.

twilliams@thestreet.com

You've become a Super Searcher in the course of working as an editor and writer. To start out, tell me about the magazine and your role there.

Upside [221, see Appendix A] is an irreverent business technology magazine that's about 10 years old. It covers the business of high technology for executives, senior level technology managers, and investors. We do company profiles and interviews and cover business trends from what I'd call a skeptical perspective with a little edge of humor. The magazine is monthly. We add new information daily to our Web site, which we call UpsideToday. We have above 150,000 subscribers and are a controlled-circulation magazine.

Upside is more of a business publication than a trade publication. The reader is looking at the magazine and our Web site for our particular *Upside* perspective. By that, I mean that what we write about is not hype-driven, as is much of the rest of the industry. We don't cover companies because they're trendy at the moment. I expect that our audience would gain an understanding of how a company does business and whether it's interesting from the articles we write.

The monthly magazine gives panoramas of the high-tech industry and profiles industry leaders. Investors definitely use the information to gauge whether they agree with the CEO's philosophy or not. Executives garner management tips and assess whether they believe in the fundamentals of a company based on what they're saying and how we're portraying them within the industry.

At the Web site, UpsideToday, we have a morning update called the "Executive Briefing" that includes major industry events. The Executive Briefing provides our readers with information about hot companies and companies that have products, cultures, and management styles that would mesh with their own interests. I would go so far as to say that we provide a forum for the technology elite, if you will.

My working title is Senior Editor and Senior Writer for both the monthly magazine and the Web site. I write a daily column on the Web and am in charge of the editorial side of things there. We have a couple of staff reporters and many freelance writers whom I oversee. I've been at *Upside* for about three and a half years. The publisher asked me to create and manage the daily Web site in March 1998. I include stock market coverage, news, profiles, and opinion pieces. Up until then, they were running an occasional magazine article as well as some news updates at the site. What I'm doing now provides much more.

What is your educational background and what did you do before coming to *Upside*?

I graduated from Stanford in 1994 as a history major but without any business background at all. During college, I worked on the school paper for three years and wrote a daily column. After graduation, my dad gave me a big stack of *Upside* issues, and I thought it was great.

My first job out of college was for Ryan Hankin Kent, a telecommunications consulting firm. They have technical analysts who conduct market research and write large, 250-page type market analyst reports about fiber-optic components and fiber channel, high-speed storage and media services. I worked with many of their analysts to produce reports. This involved interviewing them and writing and interpreting what they were trying to say, because a lot of it was very technical and hard to get across. Basically, I would take what the engineers said and make it understandable. I went straight from being a history major at school to writing about fiber optics, and it was very exciting.

I was at Ryan Hankin Kent for a year and a half, and then worked at Smart Valley, a nonprofit organization that is now defunct. I wrote manuals describing things such as how to wire up school networks.

What are some of your research responsibilities?

A lot of the research I do involves fact-checking. To do fact-checking, you highlight every fact in an article—everything that could be proven wrong, anything that's not opinion. Then you check things like the full company name, location, dates, and times. If the writer quotes from an article, you jump on Lexis-Nexis [127] and make sure that the quote is correct. The monthly magazine has a three-month lead-time for articles, whereas, on the Web, I turn stories around in two or three hours and have to work quickly. It becomes much more difficult to check everything.

In the last year, I've had to learn how to find information on the Web as well as on Lexis-Nexis, which I use for verifying facts for many of the stories submitted to me as senior editor. I also check and double-check all the financial information we use. It's necessary to check historical and current stock quotes, especially from stories written by opinion columnists. A columnist who writes about a very fuzzy topic, say a penny stock, but within a larger context, may talk about how certain stocks have lost half their value in the last year, and that the peso is involved in that. He or she doesn't necessarily have financial background in the market. I need to track back and make sure that the stock's behavior over the last year, or the last couple of years, has been portrayed accurately.

One site that I like in particular is StockSite, which is part of Silicon Investor [203]. It has both an historical and a real-time service and is easy to use and free. You can type in the dates and get to what you want very quickly. Ease of use is important to me because I have to work so quickly. I also use Quote.com [182], an independent company located in Mountain View, California.

What other online sources do you use for your research?

I find almost all the information I need on the Web. I look at about 20 different sites every morning and select the good information of interest to our readers. I'll look at the *Seattle Times* [195] site since it usually has the best stories on Microsoft and that geographic area. In fact, I look at all the regional newspapers where major high-tech companies are located. I find that daily newspapers on the Web are a tremendous source for important information.

After I check all the sites of interest, I write a one-paragraph summary for our Web site and link to the stories. We also have the Reuters [188] wire and the Internet Wire [118] and can reuse articles from these for two weeks at our Web site.

To gather information about events and conferences, we use Yahoo! [240]. You can go to Yahoo! and type in "events" and click on "Computers and the Internet," or any of many other categories, for a list of conferences and other events of interest. The Yahoo! Finance [241] site has an amazing amount of financial information. I write a morning stock market report, and it's really nice to be able to find everything I need fairly easily, with discussion about stock upgrades and downgrades, the national markets, and anything else that's going on. For answers to particular questions, the search engine I probably use the most is Google [92].

With regard to research sources and tools, could you comment on using free sources versus commercial databases that charge fees?

Ease of use is more important than whether something is free. I find that many of the Web sites are fast and easy to use, and I don't want to have to manage an account or the passwords that come with fee-based sites. I want to be able to just type in what I need at a URL and get what I need quickly. Speed is very important to me. At some point, it might not all be free on the Web, but I kind of doubt that, at least for a lot of the information I need.

What type of research do you do for your own articles?

For my articles, I'm interested in raising issues. I'm also trying to determine whether there are new trends in an industry that investors or others will have to start accepting. I do a lot of fishing around (which is one way to describe it) because, on our news page, I try to provide only news that our readers will really be interested in. For an article about drkoop.com and AOL, I found out that drkoop.com paid $89,000,000 to have its content featured on AOL, and I wondered why the business development team was going after deals that cost so much and how reasonable it was for them to pay that dollar amount. I began a further investigation by going to the drkoop.com site, where I found a list of their partners, some of whom are major companies. That led me to wonder if they had paid such large sums for all or any of their other partnerships. Since I knew that drkoop.com had just gone public, I went to the SEC Web site [196] and looked up the drkoop.com S-1 and IPO (initial public offering) prospectus, which all new companies file when they register as public companies. It turned out they had only paid for one other deal. Basically, as I was developing the story, I was trying to find out whether what they paid AOL seemed reasonable. I could easily have found that other deals did not as cost much, and that AOL, with its captive audience of 18 million people, might have been worth $89,000,000. But I also found that they had some other deals and didn't have to pay that kind of money.

Tell me about some of your searching techniques.

I've definitely become a better researcher in recent times by using a combination of what's on the Web and other online services. I use alternate terms or crazy tangential terms that actually help me get better results. When I'm searching for events, one technique that works well is searching on an actual event rather than a category in Yahoo!, especially if I'm not sure what the category is. If I search on "Comdex," for example, which is the biggest technology event every year, I find the category and click back to broader categories under which it is listed to find other, similar events. Basically, if you follow the tree roots up the trunk, you find what you are looking for. This is something that you learn to do over time; it's working backwards, in a way.

Do you participate in electronic discussion groups on the Internet?

One site that I find very useful for investment discussions is Silicon Investor. People talk purely tech stocks and, in fact, Silicon Investor calls itself the world's largest financial discussion site. It's where rumors get started or are discussed. They also talk about management strategies; it's quite high-level and not as juvenile as other discussion groups. They may talk about the earnings of a company, and you can see what people think the outcome of certain events will be. It's a good place to get ideas for writing stories. Another similar site is Raging Bull [183].

What are some of your favorite Internet sites?

I like *The New York Times* [163] site for an all-news perspective. Another site that I find useful is Media Central [142], which is geared to both media and marketing professionals. The news page there has a section for television and cable, and I'm a cable junkie. Generally, I'm looking for stories that many of the larger sites don't pick up. At Media Central, I found a story about Rupert Murdoch getting married that other sites didn't cover. Some of our readers might be interested to know about this because they may actually be colleagues and will want to send a gift. Another great site is TheStreet.com [214]. It has some of the best investment information out there for the small investor.

How has the Internet changed your life?

If I think about how I used to find information, it was primarily by telephone. As a reporting bulldog, I would get on the phone for almost everything. Now, I can use email and the Web to open a few doors. This is a nice luxury for a reporter. You don't necessarily have to call to get background information to start a story, but instead can figure it all out yourself from articles and the Web. If you think about what it took to get microfiche for SEC filings or newspaper stories in the past, it was a big headache.

It sounds as though you use reliable sources, but what kinds of factors do you watch for with regard to quality and reliability?

This is one of a couple of burning issues. In Silicon Investor and other chat rooms, many comments that are made are an immediate red flag. You don't know who's speaking and nothing is from official sources or correspondence. There have been some great media debates about people who post fake earnings reports and fake press releases. I actually have to do a fair amount of double-checking and doubling back to figure out whether our writers have used a credible source.

Finding the numbers for stocks in more than one source is also important. You begin to get a sixth sense about whether the information looks fishy to you, whether it doesn't look very right. In those cases, I go to a few different places to see what I can find out. At one time, I used to look at some of the more obscure Web pages that were often put up by individuals. I don't do that much anymore, because I found myself looking at information that I couldn't verify. It's a waste of time. I try to start out with sources that I think are reliable from the get-go. If you look at something like Yahoo! Finance, you know they get all their data from the same source as, say, CNBC [35]—or from Morningstar [149] or Zacks Investment Research [242], which are reliable and well-known companies that provide information about the stock market.

What push or alerting services do you use?

I get email from a number of different sources, and I use CompanySleuth [41] to alert me about a dozen of the bellwether stocks, including companies like Microsoft, Hewlett-Packard, and IBM. CompanySleuth sends daily alerts about new SEC filings, patents and trademarks, when a company is mentioned in some of the financially-oriented chat groups, and when there is a new analyst's report on a company. I mainly get information about blue chip and Internet stocks; when any of these move, there's going to be news to report.

What new opportunities have you seen because of the Internet?

The Internet has really opened up the field of journalism. I've become what I call an "Internet journalist." There were far fewer options for work when I graduated than now. I have a couple of friends who are more need-driven, and they work for *The Washington Post*. But I find that the world of Internet journalism has opened up new opportunities, although I did see a list ranking what could be considered a media food chain, and "Internet journalist" was at the bottom, but that's okay with me. Soon we're going to see something like the French Revolution and the face of the world will be forever changed.

As far as *Upside* magazine is concerned, the Internet is just wonderful for us. For a story on the 20 most inflated technology stocks, for example, we were able to keep up on the stock price swings and ensure that the article was current by using the Web.

Aside from all the news you research and read daily, how do you keep current about what's going on as a professional in your field?

I attend major trade shows like Comdex and Internet World, as well as some executive-based conferences. When I go to a conference, I usually have to cover events and conference sessions for the magazine and I'll listen to speeches, which is a great way to keep up. What everyone is talking about at conferences is what's going to happen soon or be the big disappointment a couple of months down the road. Conferences are important because you find out what people are doing right in the moment, whereas by following the news alone, you're reading about what's happened in the past.

You need to keep a balance by both reading the news and picking up on new information at conferences as a way to find out what's to come. One of the problems with following only the news is that you're relying on journalists. A lot of news Web sites are built fairly quickly and you could be depending on the perspective of someone who may not be that well entrenched within the industry. Attending conferences provides balance and perspective and potential trends to watch for and track. It's a forward-looking way of keeping up.

What publications do you read?

I read all the local newspapers and follow C|Net's News.com [36], TheStreet.com, *The New York Times*, and *The Wall Street Journal* [226]. I also use CNN Financial [37], and we have two televisions at our office that have CNBC's financial news going all day long. This can be very helpful when I'm writing the morning or afternoon report. CNBC has been doing financial news programs for ten years and has a very knowledgeable staff.

What are your recommendations or cautionary tales for people just starting out?

Fools. Fools! But seriously, I think that this question goes back to knowing good sources and what sources to check. In one case, I was able to use Lexis-Nexis to catch what I'll call "accidental" plagiarism. We had a freelancer who had someone else take notes for him, and that person included an article in the notes. The writer didn't know that the article was copied from somewhere else, and so cut and pasted a paragraph or two into his story without quoting and citing it. Something about it sounded familiar to me. I was alerted, too, because of a difference in writing style. I knew where to go to check on it. Knowing your sources and their reliability and how to track something down to check for accuracy is very important.

What are a few of your favorite research tips?

I like to use some print reference books like *Hoover's* [95] for company profiles and *Nelson's* [158] to identify who is writing equity research reports for certain industries. Using *Nelson's* first is actually very helpful because, if they put a star by the name of an analyst, it means that they are recommending that particular analyst for the best coverage of a company or industry. You can usually call and ask some questions. Analysts are experts in various industries because they follow an industry all the time and talk to many of the executives. They will explain things in detail on the phone and spell out why things are moving the way they are and what could happen in the future.

Apart from this, *Upside* puts out various "Top 100" lists with the top technology executives, for example, in entertainment, investments, or venture capital. The equity analysts that we identify through *Nelson's* provide us with names of people who might fit the category of lists we are working on, and this is a great starting point for us. We do these lists once a quarter and the analysts have even been able to help with the hot 100 private companies by telling us the names of the most promising companies. Once we have the names of people or companies that they recommend, we can go to the company to ask additional questions.

I also check Web sites and conduct interviews of a company's customers and competitors to try to figure out how they pan out. You can get customer names from the companies directly, but, of course, those are going to be the people who like them. You always have to be skeptical.

What global or macro trends have changed or increased the need for investment-related research?

Both the general movement in the U.S. economy and the growth in the number of individual investors are major trends that have pushed individuals to dig into the stock market. I went home this past Christmas, and my parents and their friends were talking about stocks. This has never happened before. It used to be they'd talk about the high school football team, but now stocks are the rage. What that means is that, as a journalist in a business area, you can't get away with a sophomoric level of stock commentary anymore, because everybody already knows everything.

Of course, the Internet is a macro trend in itself. When I first worked at the telecommunications consulting firm, if we wanted to find an SEC filing on a telephone company, we contacted an office in Washington, D.C., sent them a $75 check, and they copied the filing and mailed it back to us. It took six weeks. But now, when I want to know more about a company because I read about a deal that sounds interesting, I can go into their S-1 filing and look at pre-IPO financials. I can get an IPO calendar and check for whatever is coming up and for whatever I need. I don't necessarily have to have a Bloomberg [19] box on my desk. Because of the Web, I have a large portion of the same information that was once provided only by Bloomberg for a huge fee. Now, I access all kinds of financial information, all kinds of details for my articles. This is a tremendous phenomenon. As a journalist, I can stay at least 10 steps ahead of my readers. I have to do my homework and know more than everybody else does. The Internet facilitates this process.

Super Searcher Power Tips and Wisdom

➤   Daily newspapers on the Web are a tremendous source for important information.

➤   I've become a better researcher in recent times by using a combination of what's on the Web and other online services.

➤   One technique that works well is to search on an actual event rather than a category in Yahoo! If I search on "Comdex," for example, I find the category it's in and click back to the broader categories under which it is listed. Basically, if you follow the tree roots up the trunk, you find what you are looking for ... it's like working backwards.

Janet Hartmann
Research Librarian and Registered Securities Representative

As an investment bank librarian in the Business Information Center at William Blair & Co., Janet Hartmann uses many online research services and skills to answer a wide range of complex questions.

jlh@wmblair.com

Could you give me an overview of William Blair & Co.?

We're an investment bank located in Chicago with several areas of business, including retail and wholesale brokerage services, investment management and mutual funds, and securities research, also known as broker research reports. We also advise on mergers and acquisitions; provide financing through initial public offerings (IPOs), public debt offerings, and private placements; and supply venture capital through private equity and mezzanine structures.

A private placement is simply debt or equity that is only offered to institutional investors rather than sold on the public market. Private equity is venture capital in exchange for an equity ownership stake, whereas mezzanine means there is both equity and debt involved. We have about 800 employees and concentrate heavily on midwest companies, but do participate in national deals as well.

Tell me about your background.

I'm one member of a 10-person library. As with many people, librarianship is my second career. At one time, I was an opera stage manager. I have often been asked how I went from that to librarian. A stage manager is a little like a knowledge manager of the theater. You make sure that everybody knows what's going on—such as telling the guy constructing the tables for the bar scene that the soprano is going to stand on them—and then you write everything down and keep it forever, which is similar in a way to some library activities.

I decided to go in a different direction, began researching various jobs, and found that I liked research. I completed graduate school with a degree in library science. While in school, I worked at Continental Bank and spent almost a year as the secretary for a group of lawyers who worked on loan participations, which is when a bank sells parts of a loan to other banks. This group was also involved in derivative agreements. "Derivative" is a broad term, but the derivatives I worked on were designed to help companies hedge their interest rate risk. Afterwards, I worked for a group of bankers for a year, which was very helpful for my later research because I learned a lot, including terminology. In finance, terminology is a world of its own. In these early stages, I knew what the words meant but didn't necessarily know where to find the information required, whereas a lot of librarians come out of library school knowing which sources to use, but with little idea about what a lot of it means.

After I graduated from Chicago's Rosary College in 1993 with my master's degree, I was hired by the library at Continental Bank. I stayed there for several years. Working in the bank's library was like working in a research mill. I spent about 99 percent of my time doing research on seemingly every topic and industry. Only about 30 percent of the research specifically involved banking questions. I was working with a team of very experienced searchers, so this was great exposure for a newcomer like me.

In 1996, I co-chaired a committee for the Illinois Special Libraries Association (SLA) research service at the Democratic National Convention. My co-chair was the Library Manager at William Blair, and, when a position opened, I applied and was hired. My research here is much more of a mix of investment information combined with information about companies and industries. Many questions have to do with statistics and financial data.

What qualifications do you need to work in an investment research setting?

You must have online research skills and know about the financial world. One interesting aspect to my job is that I'm a registered securities representative, which requires that one take a Series 7 Exam from the National Association of Securities Dealers (NASD) [155, see Appendix A]. NASD gives a number of exams for people who participate in the investment industry. Series 7 is the most general. Every broker and sales assistant has to pass the Series 7 test. If you're a supervising broker, or a principal of a firm, or specialize in futures and options, you have to have more advanced licenses. Almost all the research librarians at William Blair voluntarily take the Series 7 exam because it educates you about industry regulations. The investment world is highly regulated and everyone wants to be in compliance and not break a rule, even accidentally. Studying for the exam is also valuable because it teaches you a lot of the terms and about the structure of financial markets. The class lasts for six weeks, two nights a week, and then you have a couple of weeks off to study before taking the test, which is about three hours. It's not as rigorous as taking an exam for the CFA (Chartered Financial Analyst) or the bar.

Could you talk more about what you learn in this course and why it's so useful to your work as a researcher?

You learn exactly how stocks are traded on the auction market—in that big noisy room in New York. This is where buyers and sellers bid and the "specialist" maintains order. You also learn about the over-the-counter electronic markets, where the "market maker" posts bid and ask prices and then matches up the orders he receives. It seems so chaotic, and yet it all gets done in seconds.

The course includes a discussion about what happened in the '30s after the 1929 crash and the laws passed in response to the crash. This explains why the investment industry is regulated the way it is. You learn about different types of securities, like the difference between a stock and a bond, details about customer accounts and processing procedures, and how options work. Particularly useful are explanations about economic indicators such as the GDP (gross domestic product), employment figures, industrial production, and capacity utilization—and why these are important and how they move the market.

The purpose of a prospectus is another subject that's covered. When a company offers stock for the first time, it writes a very detailed prospectus and files a form S-1 with the Securities and Exchange Commission (SEC) [196]. These filings contain valuable information on the company and the industry and are used to help make investment decisions. The next time the company offers stock, they don't have to include as much in the prospectus. The IPO prospectuses can provide a lot of information about the company, and the industry information can provide clues to the best sources for industry statistics, even if the prospectus is too dated to use the actual numbers.

It sounds like what you learn while studying for the NASD exam makes a difference in your ability to do good research.

You make a good point. That background, plus the work experience in the industry, and being an individual investor—all contribute to doing good research. Those entering the field as information professionals or researchers must have some basic understanding. This type of specialized industry knowledge is not a part of a person's everyday life. Unless you learn something about the field, you can't intuit where to find information about markets and investments, who has that information and why, or what information is not going to be available.

Unfortunately, you can't take the Series 7 course until you get a job with a broker. But you can buy the textbooks. Mine is from Dearborn Financial Publishing [51]. Books such as *The Wall Street Journal Guide to Understanding Money and Investments* [227] are useful for gaining an understanding of the industry. The New York Institute of Finance's [159] series—*How the Stock Market Works, How the Bond Market Works,* and others—contain more detailed descriptions.

I know that you've been doing online research for more than seven years now. Would you tell me about some of the key vendors and databases you use and their applications?

For many company and industry searches, I use some of the same standby sources that general business researchers use. I'll pull an annual report or a D&B [58] Credit Report, do a news search on a company, or start with Dialog [52] databases for industry information, such as Business & Industry [24], PROMT [178], and the Gale Group Trade & Industry Database [87].

What's nice about working at an investment bank is that, generally, online cost is not the major concern. I'm very fortunate to have worked in two very well-supported information centers. Quality of information and speed are the proverbial two out of three criteria that are usually our priority. For instance, I will often search Lexis-Nexis [127], Dow Jones [56], and Dialog, whereas if I wanted to keep the expenses down, I might select just one of these services. Most of the time, however, it's necessary to go into depth and often find everything we can.

For other types of searches, I do use specialized sources. One major vendor geared to the investment industry is FactSet Data Services [71]. Basically, they provide an interface for financial information that is in turn supplied by companies such as Compustat [43], Value Line [223], and others. These companies provide stock prices, financial statements, and other statistical information. Through the FactSet interface, we use data from Compustat, for example, to screen for companies in a particular industry or that meet certain financial criteria. Compustat takes data from 10-Ks and standardizes it. A 10-K is the annual report filed by most public companies with the Securities and Exchange Commission; it provides a comprehensive overview of the registrant's business. The report must be filed within 90 days after the end of the company's fiscal year. Although the same basic information is required for all companies, the line items and accounting treatment may differ from 10-K to 10-K. Compustat creates a database in which every company's income statement is figured in the same way and uses exactly the same financial items. There are hundreds of financials; FactSet is a powerful tool that we use frequently. The FactSet interface also allows you to use Excel templates containing stock tickers and selected data codes. I particularly like FactSet because of the consistency across companies and because you can use the Excel templates over and over for every deal. FactSet's purpose is to supply standardized data that facilitates comparing companies to each other. However, when you need the "as reported" financial statement numbers, you have to go back to the 10-K.

Would you explain what you mean by "screening for companies"?

Screening involves selecting and entering criteria to find similar companies. Many tools on the Internet and on company CD-ROM products allow you to screen, but FactSet stands out for its functionality and sheer number of data items. You can ask for all the companies in a particular SIC code with sales greater than a certain amount, with a P/E ratio (price divided by earnings per share) less than a certain amount, and a debt-to-equity ratio less than a particular percentage. The system comes back with all companies that match your criteria and up pop the names on your screen.

We use FactSet in all our departments—corporate finance, debt finance, and private equity—to find information on comparable companies. Comparables, or comps, just means similar companies for comparison. A research analyst or investment manager may be comparing P/E and margins; a private equity or M&A analyst may be comparing purchase price to cash flow or EBITDA multiples (earnings before interest, taxes, depreciation, and amortization). It's all related to the valuation of a company and setting a fair price based on what others have paid for similar businesses.

Other databases we use for finding comparables are Securities Data Corp. (SDC) [199] and Mergerstat [144], two competitors that provide large databases of mergers and acquisitions deals. Again, you can screen for what you need by selected variables. For example, you may want to find companies in a particular SIC code, and deals over 50 million dollars, where 50 percent stock and 50 percent cash was paid. The database might come up with a list of a hundred deals. You can download information about them. We use these types of databases all the time and we can really produce fast results. SDC also has databases of equity and debt offerings, stock buybacks, bankruptcies, and venture capital investments.

What other major databases do you use?

One key source is CDA/Spectrum [32], which is under the umbrella of Thomson Financial Securities Data (TFSD) [215]. CDA/Spectrum is a database of institutional and insider owners with information garnered from SEC Form 3, Form 4, Form 13, and Form 13-F. Forms 3 and 4 name insiders, and 13-F contains the names of institutions. The 13-Ds list those who own five percent of a stock. CDA/Spectrum takes information from all these filings and builds a database. You can key in a company name and find out all the institutional owners or key in an institution and find out what companies they own.

You can also find names of various stocks and who owns all of them. This is very handy for identifying names of major shareholders. When our company is planning a road show to market a secondary offering, we can find investors who already own the stock. When we are planning a road show for an IPO, we can learn who owns other companies in the same industry.

Also, we may want to discuss major shareholders with a client. Occasionally, when an announced acquisition is undergoing a contentious vote, the major shareholders may be contacted to measure their support.

CDA/Spectrum merged with Technimetric, which was their competitor in this field. The data for both companies are being combined into one database.

Another database that I use all the time is the SEC on Primark Global Access [53]. I feel lucky that we have an account with Global Access, which is an expensive service, but fast and effective to use. More than 100 people here have Global Access on their desktops. Sometimes, I must generate a large amount of information. Our department might be asked to verify details about 50 or 100 merger deals in an afternoon. Each librarian here will work with a list of, say, 20 companies. In a situation like this, I don't want to use the free EDGAR Internet systems because they may not respond quickly enough or have the same functionality as Global Access. Global Access has a wonderful search interface and allows you to send results to a Word document that looks beautiful—with all the page breaks in the right places and columns for tables not wrapping around to the next line—and that you can email directly to users.

One feature of Global Access that I couldn't do without is its index and image documents of all the non-EDGAR filings. You don't get these on the free Internet EDGAR services. For me, it's critical to have a system that identifies non-EDGAR filings for looking up older deals that often appear in a list of comparable companies. We may want to pull filings from deals from as long as 10 years ago. I've also done some oddball projects; for example, one in which I had to find out what SEC documents said about the relationship between dual classes of stock and the price disparity between the two classes. A complete description of how the classes work might be found in one of the pre-EDGAR filings. For example, a company such as J.M. Smucker has Class A stock and Class B stock. TCI has Class A and Class B; that's another example. Usually, there's a difference in the two classes—for instance, in the number of votes each gets or how dividends are paid. A Class A shareholder may get 10 votes for every 1 vote that a Class B shareholder gets. Or maybe the Class B shareholders get no votes, but get preferential dividend treatment. A price gap between the two classes will reflect these differences. If you're trying to set a valuation for a company with two classes of stock, it's important to see all the other examples of similar situations.

Another way in which companies issue more classes of stock is in a situation called targeted stock. A good example of that is General Motors, which has the GM Hughes "H" stock and which used to have the "E" stock, which was for EDS (Electronic Data Services). A targeted stock is a particular class of stock that's used to track the performance of a subsidiary.

On the subject of EDGAR, do you have any other hints or tips to add?

My main comment is to reiterate that one should not depend solely on a free EDGAR-only database. The non-EDGAR filings can be important. For instance, amendments to 10-Ks don't have to be filed in EDGAR. Many companies do it anyway, but you could miss something important. Also, some ownership filings are not required to be filed electronically either, and sometimes the last proxy before a merger is non-EDGAR.

What public records databases do you use?

One company I'd like to mention is Information America [104] because their Internet products are a big improvement over their old proprietary software. They offer the Informed Investigator and Informed Lender series, which we get and which are for heavy users. We search them for bankruptcies, lawsuits, liens and judgements, and UCC (Uniform Commercial Code) filings and "skip tracers." Skip tracers are databases that allow you to search by name or social security number to find all the addresses used by an individual.

We do a lot of background checks, especially for the private equity and corporate finance departments. Private equity companies and IPO candidates are usually small and haven't been in the public eye very much. Little is known about who the people are and where they came from. Background checks are needed for just about every deal. We search all the news and public records databases to verify the information a company has provided us and to make sure there aren't any skeletons in anybody's closet. It's part of our responsibility to our investors.

Information America has an Internet product for occasional users called KnowX [126]. I have also used public records on Lexis-Nexis and CDB-InfoTek [33]. We use more than one public records vendor because they all have different coverage in terms of the states, counties, and date ranges they include. It gets to be fairly difficult to keep track of who covers what. For national coverage, I don't think you need to search all systems, but generally at least two.

Could you talk about data quality issues?

As an investment bank, we must have—and know how to get—pristine data. Often, we take the reports we get from an SDC search and go to Global Access, which provides actual SEC documents. We pull all the original SEC documents, which are used by the corporate finance department to verify all the numbers that are generated by the databases we use. The firm must write a letter to the shareholders of an acquired company and tell them that the deal has been examined and weighed against comparable deals, and that it's believed to be a fair deal for the price. Before the letter is written, an investment bank must make sure that the information used for the evaluation of the deal is correct information. We on the library staff supply the documents containing the merger agreement and the financials of the target, if they've been filed. They are often with the 8-K, a filing of "material event." Acquisitions or divestitures that meet the SEC tests of significance must be filed (the SEC's tests of significance are complicated, but a good rule of thumb is that below

10 percent of the assets or sales of the seller, or the acquirer is not going to require much disclosure), but can also be attached to a prospectus, registration statement, proxy, or even a 10-K or 10-Q. Sometimes more information, such as the target's financial statements, is filed in another 8-K months after the deal.

Part of my job involves digging around to locate all these documents, and printing out sometimes hundreds of pages. If the merger is not significant enough to merit separate filings, we use the full-text searching function on Global Access to find any mention of the deal in any of the company's documents. Even a paragraph in a 10-K that confirms the price paid and gives the target's revenues is better than no information. Failing that, we look for company press releases.

I give all the pieces of information and filings to the corporate finance or private equity departments, who read them and compare financials from the various sources. They pore over the numbers to ensure accuracy of our comparables list. In fact, financial firms have a whole set of people who work with these documents. Between their undergraduate degrees and the time they go back for an M.B.A. and then go to work in corporate settings, they spend two or three years at an investment bank, private equity firm, or commercial bank, depending on their interests. This is where they get number-crunching experience.

As I mentioned, part of my job is to pull all the pieces and source documents together to support those who are involved in this aspect of quality control. A lot of my work is like that of a detective, trying to find out where the company actually put either a document or piece of information. Both SDC and Mergerstat have significant quality problems. From what I know, the problem lies in the systems and how they gather data. The disclosure information is sometimes not filed in an obvious place because it's attached to something else later on, and database information is initially entered from SEC filings or from press releases and news articles. After that, additional filings—noting adjustments to the pricing or structure, or adding the target financials—are not always picked up. That's why we do these time-consuming searches of the actual SEC database.

Another problem is in searches conducted at the end of a year. I may find that the volume of mergers for the previous year is completely different in each online system. Each has slightly different criteria for inclusion and different ways of calculating data. SDC and Mergerstat contain information reported in the newspapers, but their figures are hard to reproduce through other original sources.

I don't want to completely disparage these companies for their quality. But when you're going to sign your name to something, you must check and double-check the numbers. If all you need is a general idea, it's fine to use these as very quick ways to get information. Starting from scratch and using the SEC database to generate a list of comparable deals would be a nightmare, if not completely impossible. Once a list of comps is generated, you can then go to the SEC filings with names and dates for perhaps 30 or 40 filings, instead of searching all of EDGAR for the word "merger" and sorting through hundreds and hundreds and hundreds of filings.

It sounds as though you're not having problems with data integrity but must perform extra checks to be sure to get the data right.

Yes. Another point that can affect quality is that, for a long time, SDC had no serious competitors. Mergerstat published an annual print volume and a print transaction roster, but they didn't have an electronic database. Now they do, and it's available on Lexis-Nexis and also from Data Downlink's .xls service [48] on the Internet. Now that SDC has a much more visible competitor, maybe we'll see improvements; at least, that's the hope.

What are some of the print or CD-ROM reference tools you use?

We want to have as many directories as possible that describe venture capital and buyout firms such as Kohlberg Kravis Roberts, which assembles multimillion-dollar investment funds to invest in individual companies through equity stakes and buyouts. This type of firm doesn't have to disclose a lot of information publicly, and no one source captures information about all of them. We have half a dozen directories to help us identify these firms. Some are CD-ROMs and others are in print.

A company called Asset Alternatives, Inc. publishes *Galante's Venture Capital and Private Equity Directory* [85] and *The Private Equity Analyst* newsletter [177]. *Galante's* is one of the major directories and comes in both print and CD-ROM. *Pratt's Guide to Venture Capital Sources* [175], published by SDC, is a directory of venture capital firms originally published by Shannon Pratt, who also writes a newsletter and wrote the valuation classic, *Valuing a Business.* We use another SDC book called the *Directory of Financing Buyout Sources.* SDC also has databases for venture capital firms, venture-backed companies, and venture funds. Another company called Venture One [224] produces a database called Venture Source, which is accessed over the Internet. It lists the financial firms and also, uniquely, indicates names of companies in which they invest, which is very helpful. Fitzroy Dearborn publishes the *International Directory of Venture Capital Funds* [113].

What specific kinds of questions do you answer with these directories?

One question I'm asked fairly regularly is, "What companies are investing in a particular industry?" I may gather a list of a couple hundred firms and then select by criteria, such as size, to cut the list down. I include a company profile that describes the company, what it has done, whom it has invested in, and who the important people in the company are. These companies are possible buyers for a company that our firm may be offering for sale.

Companies put themselves up for sale for several reasons. Sometimes, a company grows to the point where it just can't grow anymore without some capital. Sometimes, a company is just not doing well, and the shareholders get annoyed and want the company sold to somebody else. At times, an industry consolidates because there are too many competitors and no one's doing well. From time to time, you'll see a press release that describes how a company has engaged an investment bank such as William Blair to "explore strategic options." This means that it is trying to sell the company.

Let's talk about the Internet and its effect on you as a researcher.

In thinking about the Internet, the first thing that pops into my head is government information. In the pre-Internet days, government information was especially difficult to get. You'd have to call an agency, and you could often tell that whomever you were talking to probably did not want to help you much. Sometimes, you almost had to plead. Then you had to wait, sometimes for a couple of days. You'd call again, trying not to be a pest but still nagging for something you needed. This has all changed; now, you just pop onto whatever government Internet site you need.

The same is true for associations. It's wonderful. You just go and get that PDF file and the job is done in five minutes. This is such a huge improvement in my work life. I also love using the Internet to telnet to commercial services instead of dialing in. Because of our network with T-1 lines, it's faster to work through an Internet connection than with dial-up.

Have you found any financially-oriented Web sites or search engines that are particularly important?

There's Venture One, which I've mentioned. The Mutual Fund Café [154] is unique. Financial Research Corporation [76] and some other mutual fund consulting companies are sponsors. It has original articles on trends, mergers and acquisitions activity, and statistics in the mutual fund industry. Other than these, there aren't a lot of Internet sites established enough to replace the commercial services in providing information, particularly for the financial markets.

I've seen some Internet sites that are "venture communities," where people who wish to invest and people who want to raise capital post messages. These are supposed to be networks where people find each other. We don't use this type of source because of concerns about who's out there and whether he or she is credible. However, people in that world who are looking for names may find that these sites are a starting point, as long as they verify the information they find.

Stock research Web sites are problematic to me because they are so many steps away from the primary data. A site may have Hoover's Company Profiles [95] and also use Media General [143] for financials. They both get their data from the SEC, but the more times it's processed, the more chances for error and confusion. You just can't be sure of the quality of the numbers and how current they are. Have they adjusted everything for splits? Have they incorporated the most recent quarterly release? I tend to stick to sources such as FactSet, which clearly states what's included and what's adjusted. Creating accurate and current databases is labor-intensive, and access to them is expensive, but for our purposes, the costs are justified.

For search engines, I use AltaVista [3] and HotBot [96] for broad coverage, and Google [92] because results pop to the top quickly. Sometimes, I use the Internet, not so much as a source, but as another method of access. After a standard search using tried and true databases, I may use Northern Light [167]. I let its relevancy algorithm go to work. I would never do this instead of Boolean searching, because I don't trust Web search engines enough. But when I don't have a clue about the topic, or when I don't know what a technical term means, an Internet search can help me become educated quickly. I also like to double-check to see what serendipity will bring to the top. You can sometimes find some gems if you let yourself go a little.

When do you use a commercial source instead of the Internet, and vice versa?

The major commercial services have moved their paid systems onto the Web, but some of the HTML interfaces are horrible and clunky, so I still use the classic interfaces for many of them. One commercial vendor I use instead of free Internet sites is Haver Analytics [94], a company that provides a lot of government statistics. Haver now has an Internet interface and the contract cost commitment is moderate. Using Haver is both fast and affordable. The cost is $3-10 for each time series, no matter how far back you go. They primarily cover government statistics and some private information, such as home sales data from the National Association of Realtors, which collects that type of information, and data from the Consumer Confidence Index provided by the Conference Board. A similar source, DRI [57] from McGraw-Hill, also offers time series data that you can download. Every permutation of each series is already done for you. DRI does require a sizable annual contract.

If I didn't use Haver, I would have to go to different government Web sites for the same information that Haver puts together in one spreadsheet. With the government sites, it's necessary to pull information from various ASCII documents, paste the data into a spreadsheet, and combine information from several spreadsheets into one. If somebody wants the whole PCE (Personal Consumption Expenditures) breakdown tabulated by the Bureau of Economic Analysis [22] for the last month only, then I'll use the government Web site because they have a press release with just that information. I also use the White House Economic Statistics Briefing Room [234], and I have bookmarked many of the government sites that provide statistics that people repeatedly ask for—the CPI (Consumer Price Index), population data from the U.S. Bureau of the Census [218], and housing data, for example.

On the other hand, if someone wants the PCE for the home furnishings segment and the home repairs segment, plus the GDP and the unemployment rate, all quarterly for the last 30 years, then I go to Haver and download the entire time series. It's more cost-effective than spending the time at each government site, finding the correct time series, downloading it, then pasting it into a spreadsheet and combining all four.

I use Haver for questions from analysts who need to compare economic statistics relevant to the company or industry they are working on. Some of the analysts cover financial firms, such as banks and credit card companies, and closely follow the savings rates, consumer debt, or bankruptcy statistics. Haver also has a push system called DLX that pops up daily with the most up-to-date information available; I can put this information right into a spreadsheet and produce the graphs.

Are there other situations in which you would go to the Internet first instead of a commercial online system?

Sometimes, I get requests for an important piece of current news. In one case, an analyst might hear that a local paper has done a negative story on a company he's interested in. I go to the newspaper's Web site and, as early as 7:30 in the morning on the day the paper is published, can find what I'm looking for. You can't always find the most current day for local papers on the commercial database services. On the other hand, if I'm told that a news story could have appeared during the past three months, I use Dow Jones or Lexis-Nexis because I don't want to go to every Web site to search every newspaper individually.

I also find that a lot of companies put valuable information on their Web pages. I was researching a company that is in the business of investing in other companies. One of our brokers wanted a list of the companies they invest in. I looked in the SEC filings and would have had to pull this information from 10 documents to make up a list. Instead, I found all the desired information conveniently located on the company's Web site.

Sometimes, a private company's site has a huge amount of information that you would never have found in the old days. In order to make people comfortable with them and to sell products, a company will post all kinds of information. That's great. This was impossible before the advent of the Web. Some sites are gems. It's amazing what people will put up. If you called and asked them for that information, they would say no.

Do you have to be extra careful because companies are putting up unaudited or unanalyzed information?

First of all, it's important to be sure that what you are looking at is actually the company's Web site. I like to verify Web sites in another source, such as one of our company directories. A lot of company directories are starting to list URLs. It's also useful to have Alexa [2] running, because you can see the name and address of the site's registrant. Alexa is software that you can download; it works with your Internet browser to provide some basic information about each site.

It's important to know that you shouldn't use the information you find at Web sites without some kind of verification process. With private companies, you've got to get everything you can and evaluate what matches up. If the company talks about sales, you're certainly going to want to take that with a shaker of salt. When they're describing products or giving biographies of their executives, it's a little more concrete and less suspect.

What is your experience with electronic discussion groups?

I have a great Usenet story. One of our securities analysts follows H&R Block and wanted to know about the IRS preparation for the Y2K problem. All the government statements she had come across indicated that the IRS was doing fine and had no problems or concerns with regard to Y2K. She wasn't sure she could believe what she was hearing and thought there might be something else going on. I searched Usenet using Alta Vista and found a transcript from a luncheon meeting where the speaker was the head of the House Committee that oversees the IRS. He had quite a different tale to tell, saying that he thought it was going to be a disaster. I used his name to search for more Usenet articles and found many instances where he had made similar statements. My earlier search of the traditional press had not picked up these statements. The Usenet discussion group was a great starting place. I don't use discussion groups often, because all you are really getting from them are somebody's opinions, but the information I found in this instance was really valuable.

Do you use any push or alerting services?

We use NewsEdge [165], and a lot of our research analysts like products that will send them email alerts. We subscribe to about 20 sources from the NewsEdge list, including Knight-Ridder Business, which combines a number of newspapers. NewsEdge also has *Fortune, Forbes, Business Week*, the *Dow Jones Wire*, and Reuters. We set up profiles for a few of our users, but many learn how to do this on their own. We also circulate tables of contents from CARL UnCover [30]. Our users check to see if there's something important they should know about, rather than reading periodicals cover to cover.

We subscribe to technology research companies such as International Data Corporation (IDC) [112] and Forrester Research [82]. You can go to their Web sites for their reports, but they also offer email alerts on particular topics, and the analysts like this format. Those two services have particularly good systems in which the analysts get what they want without our having to do any additional filtering for them.

On a daily basis, five of us read the national and Chicago papers and scan business magazines for articles about clients or companies of interest to our various departments. We look especially for cover stories and alert the analysts before anybody calls them about what's being said.

You've mentioned using spreadsheets. What other kinds of deliverables do you provide?

I both crunch numbers and deliver end results as Word documents. The deliverables vary by project. I sometimes spend as much time preparing the finished work as I spend finding the information to begin with. When to spend a lot of time depends on the user's needs. Those working with mergers and acquisitions deals must read through all of those SEC documents, and I can't do this for them. If someone asks a qualitative question, however, I will often summarize information from articles. I'll do whatever I can to make their job easier. My reports are typically informal, sometimes an email or memo, and written with the expectation that the user will also look at the articles. We're not analysts and they can't just take our word for it. But I tell them the shape of what I'm sending, in order to help them make sense of it. No matter what you do, sometimes you can't just give them a short answer. They will have to read a lot.

How do you stay current professionally and maintain an edge so that you can do the best job for your users?

A favorite way to stay current is by participating in an electronic discussion group called BUSLIB-L [26]. I don't post much because of confidentiality issues, but I try to answer questions when I can, and I read the digest every day.

I also have a card file. It's old-fashioned, but I have a card for every industry and every finance topic, and I just jot things down and consult the file for information on a range of questions. I also receive the Scout Report [192] and the *Search Engine Watch* update newsletter [193], both delivered by email. These keep me informed about new search engines and how they change. I read *EContent* [62], *ONLINE* [172], and *Searcher* [194], because they have really good, meaty articles. I also read *Information Today* [106] to keep track of who owns whom in the information industry. I really enjoy reading the editorials by Barbara Quint.

I also read some magazines that regularly cover technology finance, like *Red Herring* [184] and *Upside* [221], and I read *Business 2.0* [23] and the *Industry Standard* [101] to keep up-to-date on technology issues. Apart from the magazines, I read the financial pages of major newspapers to keep up on what's important to the people I work for, and *Barron's* [18] and *The Economist* [60] because I want to be up on what's happening in the world.

I know that's a long list but, fortunately, I have a long train ride and am a good skimmer. I look for articles that explain or describe terminology and economic indicators because I must know more about how the CPI is calculated than the person I'm giving the information to. I also like to stay up-to-date on who is buying whom, whose stock just tanked, and what the market did yesterday. It can get exciting here when the stock market drops precipitously and the markets close for a couple of hours.

Do you have any success stories in which your research saved the day?

All of us in the library often work on a deal over the course of several weeks. In one case, we were working with a client who was a manufacturing company in Eastern Europe. Our firm was competing against another investment bank for M&A business, and, in our pitch book, we included seven comparable deals. The other investment bank only had one; this helped win the business. We had searched SDC and Mergerstat to find the information. For this type of project, you don't strictly follow the instruction booklet, so to speak, but instead have to really question how many different ways companies in an industry can be uncovered. We were able to make the firm look good, and it made our firm some business.

What do you see as global or macro trends that have changed or increased the need for investment-related research?

One trend is the global trend itself. You really can't do without international sources and knowledge about the world anymore. You have to understand the differences in public company disclosure in other countries, because it doesn't work the same as for the U.S. Primark [176] has a Web site for individual investors. When you click on "Guide to International Filings," there's a country-by-country list of filing requirements. There's also a site called CorporateInformation.com [44], which is divided by country. It includes a page called "Definitions of Identifiers and Company Extensions," which has all those company extensions like AG, GmbH or SA, and what each term means in the countries that use these abbreviations. If you didn't know that a company was German but you looked up GmbH at this site, you would know that the company is in Germany; that's a starting point for your research. It's also important to know that, in some countries, private companies must file financial information, and public records or databases are available from various sources internationally. In the U.K, all companies, whether public or private, file with the Companies House [40], for instance.

What's the best way to get filings from other countries?

If they trade at all in the U.S., even over-the-counter, you can get some information from the SEC. Otherwise, a couple of companies that can retrieve the information are Global Securities Information, Inc. [89], which does a lot of this type of document retrieval, and Global Research [88] in St. Louis, which will get you annual reports from other countries. Sometimes, we use Find/SVP's [78] foreign offices. It usually takes a few days to get international company reports, because of time differences or other reasons. It's not something you can get instantaneously the way you can SEC filings. But it's important just to know that companies in certain countries only have to file twice a year, rather than quarterly as in the U.S., so that you don't go off trying to find a third quarter report that doesn't exist. Canada's SEDAR [201] system, the equivalent of EDGAR, now has electronic filings online too, rather than just the index. SEDAR stands for System for Electronic Document Analysis and Retrieval; it's an electronic filing system for the disclosure documents of public companies and mutual funds across Canada.

Any closing thoughts?

The financial services industry is unique. With regard to research, there's a lot to learn that isn't taught in library school. In this position, I've learned more about going to the second stage. I can spend the time and money to dig deeply on most projects. After I've found articles or reports on a topic, I see who the articles quote as sources, and I track down additional primary research. When I find contradictory statistics in various articles, I call the sources and ask them about their methodology and how they differ from another source. If an association is quoted, I try to find out whether the members report actual statistics, or whether the information is from a survey and has been extrapolated to the whole industry.

When I search SDC, I look into where they get the information and which companies have to file what and when. In that way, I can understand and explain what's missing. I know how much other searchers use the information they find in prospectuses and broker reports, and I want the data that I provide to our analysts who create these reports to stand up to scrutiny over time for all users. Going deeper and adding value is something that information professionals must do.

Super Searcher Power Tips and Wisdom

➤   IPO prospectuses can provide a lot of information about companies and industries.

➤   You shouldn't use the information you find at Web sites alone without some kind of verification.

➤   I both crunch numbers and deliver end results as Word documents. I sometimes spend as much time preparing the finished work as I spend finding the information in the first place.

➤   You have to understand the differences in public company disclosure in other countries, because it doesn't work the same as in the U.S.

Richard Harrison
Investment Information Entrepreneur

Richard Harrison is co-founder and partner of Global Securities Information, Inc., the producer of LIVEDGAR, a value-added online database service that encompasses the Securities and Exchange Commission EDGAR.

rharrison@gsionline.com
www.gsioline.com

Tell me about your company, services, and clients.

Global Securities Information, Inc. (GSI) has eighteen researchers based in Washington, D.C., and a research staff located in New York. The researchers here are applications experts and very knowledgeable about SEC [196, see Appendix A] filings, documents released by other commissions, and their use. Our research services are geared toward transactional researchers (primarily lawyers and private law firms), individuals from public and private corporations, investment bankers, as well as professional information specialists like the librarians and legal assistants who work for them. We also provide services to mass and trade media business writers.

Transactional law, as opposed to litigation, involves drafting documents such as those for mergers and acquisitions, public company offerings, employee benefit plans, tax disclosure, indenture, or credit agreements. These types of documents require all the material and substantive underpinnings of press releases and other information that companies release about their activities. The purpose of filing these documents with the

SEC is to inform the SEC and, importantly, the public, of all relevant information regarding the business dealings and financial health of the reporting companies.

When a transactional researcher drafts a document, he or she tries to find what the legal and financial communities call "models" or "precedent" for comparable companies within existing documents that have already been filed. Legal writers are often looking for text-based information, whereas most of the financial people are looking for numeric-based financial comparables. Both types of information are found in the public filings available from the SEC.

Our clients use the information about comparable companies as a foundation for developing their opinions and to extrapolate their own analysis. They are looking for models that have already passed regulatory muster. In the case of initial public offerings, for example, the staff of the SEC reviews initial public offerings (IPOs) for various points of conformity to the Securities Act of 1933. Those preparing IPO documents for the SEC want models of companies that are similar to their own—either in a similar industry, or by size of the company, or based on risk factors or competition discussions that have been sufficient in the amount of disclosure required by law. "Sufficient in the amount of disclosure" refers to the balancing act that legal writers have to walk between, on the one hand, disclosing enough information to conform with the letter and spirit of the securities laws and, on the other, creating potential liability by promising things that may not be delivered in the future or disclosing competitively sensitive information about their client. The idea is that, the better prepared the document, the faster the company will go through the regulatory process, and the public offering will be made quickly and in sync with market conditions.

Here at GSI, we have a variety of means for providing information to our clients. We primarily use an online research application that we developed called LIVEDGAR [134]. We also provide on-demand research services from a variety of sources, including agencies around the world. We retrieve documents and monitor federal and state courts, executive branch agencies, Congress, self-regulatory agencies, and similar regulatory bodies around the globe. We provide document-delivery services from these entities on a request basis. Many of our clients are LIVEDGAR users; they are power researchers and very intelligent people who don't necessarily know a lot about the specifics of an industry, but do know about the framework of the law. We help them find the models they need to draw context.

Our clients can both search and retrieve information they need from the LIVEDGAR database once they have an account established with us, or we'll do the research for them. It works both ways. LIVEDGAR is not a document retrieval tool *per se* like many of the EDGAR systems on the Internet, but has many more value-added features. We have incorporated our experience and knowledge into a database with online help, research guides, and a "Research Library" that loads pre-established searches. These searches have been developed based on commonly asked research questions from our users.

For example, when you use our mergers and acquisitions database, you can search for "bear hug letters," a term of art for a letter to the board of directors or the chairman from a group that wants to buy a company. The letter basically says something like, "Now is the time we've decided we need to merge and we need your help doing it, because if we don't get your help, we're going to launch a hostile tender offer." It's a squeeze—a bear hug. LIVEDGAR has a ready-made search statement that will find all the bear hug letters, even though the term "bear hug" itself doesn't appear anywhere in the letter or in an SEC filing.

The LIVEDGAR Research Library has a section that explains what kinds of SEC form types these letters may be attached to and provides links to specific recent examples that can be used as models. Or the user can find all of the most recent bear hug letters, or customize a search by industry and load ready-made search statements that we have preformulated, and then click on "submit." This is the kind of value that we add, and it's from our knowledge of the investment field and the SEC filings and the content in them.

Here's another example. We might get a request from an employee benefits attorney trying to draft models of director equity incentive plans. Using LIVEDGAR, the attorney can locate all filings that contain director equity incentive plans. He or she can select a pre-designed search strategy with Boolean operators, proximity connectors, and parentheses placed where they belong.

The bottom line is that clients don't have to recreate the wheel. They can just submit an already-designed search. There are more than 300 different searches that are ready to load, and we add 10 to 12 new ones every week. Our clients get the most current examples without having to call us for help. When they do need help, the GSI staff knows intimately what's supposed to be disclosed, where and how filings have been used and, through experiential knowledge, what's happened in the past.

Since our business is not a mainstream information business, and many of our clients are transactional lawyers who represent investment bankers and institutional investors whose most precious commodity is time, we fulfill an important role. My goal as a researcher is to minimize the breaks in the thought process of the person using the information.

Usually, our clients are writing a business story, drafting a document, or finding comparable companies. In the past, when it was a paper-based world and filings were maintained on microfiche, you spent your time copying fiche or polling experienced people. You might find some news releases on what you needed, but that was the extent of what you could do online because there weren't specialized databases like LIVEDGAR around. You'd try to find the SEC document and order it from a service bureau or get it from the company itself, or you'd see if you had it in your in-house library. But getting it would take hours, days, or weeks. What we've done at GSI is to condense that process and bring it up to the most current and complete level possible. When clients need something, they get it in a timely way from us and can incorporate it into the work that's actually at hand.

Our services are geared to save our clients' time, since their fee structures are such that they could be billing out at $200, $400, or $600 an hour, versus the five or ten minutes of our time that it might take for selected research questions and answers. The answers that we provide make our clients at least as informed as the person they're negotiating with, and they eliminate the non-billable overhead that these firms would have to pay for conducting this type of research in-house.

Many of our clients use general legal research tools such as Lexis-Nexis [127] or Westlaw [232] to answer some of their questions. They are great for case law, but for transactional law purposes, in many instances LIVEDGAR and our on-demand research services answer the same questions much more quickly. There's an economy of scale, and the specialization we offer has tremendous benefit, especially for clients who are lawyers or investment bankers.

Currently, 10,000 online researchers use LIVEDGAR as a desktop tool. Instead of finding and faxing or sending results overnight as in the past, our clients have immediate access and the ability to create working documents by integrating information into their word processing files. Or they can immediately print out attractive documents from their Web browser. Since many are busy doing legal writing, they engage us to act confidentially on their behalf to find comparable companies and models and precedent, or to monitor the SEC filings of important events that affect a company—and subsequently, the investors.

We're not a software or database company *per se*, but we know how to use technology and have created the LIVEDGAR database to help solve problems for our clients.

Let's talk about your education and background and how you came to found your own research company.

I graduated with a Bachelor of Science in Business Administration from the University of Richmond, Virginia, in

1984. I may be one of the few people in the business world who uses all the disciplines he studied in college. Initially, I had to wear all the hats. I've applied what I learned about operations management, marketing, and personnel management. I've had to focus on qualifying, training, and retraining staff.

My first job after college was working as a researcher and business representative. I've been doing research for 14 years now. Initially, I worked for a company that did the same type of research we do today at GSI. That company was acquired by a larger, current competitor of ours. I did that for approximately a year and then went to work for two years in the D.C. office of Pillsbury, Madison, and Sutro, a San Francisco-based firm with 500 lawyers. I supported eight transactional attorneys as a legal assistant and continued to do SEC research. It was beneficial to be given questions without knowledge or background of a situation, which is often the case in research. This is how I sharpened my skills.

Of course, what's most difficult before you even start a research job is to figure out what the right question is. You often find that what you've been asked is not what is really needed. Trying to learn the right question is par for the course. After that, 90 percent of the battle is done.

I was one of the first users of the test EDGAR, a trademark of the SEC and an acronym for Electronic Data Gathering, Analysis, and Retrieval. EDGAR is the primary tool used by the SEC to accept the required compliance filings from companies and individuals. The SEC was actually the first federal regulatory agency that required companies to submit compulsory filings in electronic form.

EDGAR was created by an act of Congress in 1983 and the test phase began in 1984. Around the same time, there were two public terminals in the SEC's public reference room, and I was one of probably two or three people who actually used it during its early days to find models for transactional research. It was a much different animal than it is today. There were maybe 250 or 300 companies filing electronically at that time. Today, there are many thousands. This was a nice way to learn.

During that time I met my business partner. He worked for a research company that was a competitor of my first employer. At that time, I was also applying to graduate schools in business and law but hadn't been accepted. Interestingly, all the application forms asked a similar question: "If you had all the resources you needed, what kind of business would you start and why?" I had actually been self-employed since the age of 10. You name it and I had tried it. At one time, I owned a landscaping business, and then I got the distribution rights from a multinational brewing company based in England to import their bar towels. They made beach towels from bar towels and sold them through English-style bars and some specialty retail shops. I did this while working at the law firm and put myself through college, took flying lessons, and bought my own cars. I have always been absolutely independent.

In any event, I kept seeing this question on the various applications for graduate school regarding what type of business I would start if I could. By 1988, since I didn't have a mortgage and was not married, my partner and I decided to have a go at it, and we sat down and wrote a business plan for GSI. We believed we could deliver better service than our competitors and aggregate our knowledge to create specialized databases. I think our first computer was a Leading Edge, 12-MHz machine that cost us $1,500. It was a big investment at the time. We borrowed a small amount of money to finance ourselves and started the business in April 1988 with the same specialization we have now. Our main business was, and is, in providing models and precedent. We developed our own in-house databases for this purpose, based on our experience. Prior to using computer databases to find models, you'd ask senior partners for their memory or go to a file clerk who did form filing to get assistance. It was a very different paper world prior to online technologies, EDGAR, and LIVEDGAR.

I know you wear many hats at GSI. Would you talk specifically about your research responsibilities?

At least 50 percent of my time is spent doing research. My partner and I made a conscious effort to stay directly involved in the research part of the business, because that's where change for the future comes from, especially with regard to new services and enhancing LIVEDGAR.

In the securities industry, there are some 70 different types of forms used for filing. The forms are static, but the way they're used is dynamic. Because of tax law changes in particular, for example, people find that they can do different types of structured deals and other kinds of things besides a proxy.

What are some examples of research questions and how you answer them?

In one case, a client requires disclosure language for one of his clients, a foreign private issuer. Foreign private companies are not incorporated in the U.S. and do not maintain or calculate profits for U.S. income tax purposes. This is an important tax disclosure. Our client may have conducted online searching using the general legal research databases, but has not found anything to help him on this subject. That's one thing about the research that I do—I get the most difficult questions, those that can't be answered internally by clients or from other legal research tools that many firms subscribe to in-house.

These types of questions are particularly important because, at GSI, we save our research experiences and the knowledge base we gain from the varied questions and then incorporate new features based on them into the LIVEDGAR Research Library. We load ready-made search strategies and answers onto LIVEDGAR for questions that we get over and over again but are hard to find. Currently, we're working on a LIVEDGAR enhancement based on statistical questions about financial advisors for every proxy contest—which involves change of control—that we can find from 1990 to the present. Clients need statistics about financial advisors who have been successful in these proxy contests, in which a dissident group directly solicits the shareholders.

In another type of research project, an employee benefits attorney requires examples of employment agreements in the software industry, with the name of the general counsel identified for each company. The client wants to retain an expert and also use models from other companies for negotiation. LIVEDGAR can filter by employment agreements and by industry. I can also add proximity operators to the search to get at those filings that contain the title "General Counsel." For this question, I found 30 companies that met all the parameters.

Other questions I answer cover a type of data mining for business reporters. A significant number of public companies are followed by both analysts and local business reporters, but a lot of companies are not. In those situations, the SEC filings are the first substantive point of public release for important disclosures, such as SEC investigations, either by formal or informal order. This is rather like a tax audit situation. One situation suggests you are being audited because you had a slight discrepancy in reporting. Another situation might suggest fraud, in which case a more formal investigation would be appropriate.

I can use LIVEDGAR to monitor investigations for all companies as their filings are released and create a search statement that defines both formal and informal orders of investigation. In general, the small business issuers whose capitalization is less than 25 million dollars don't typically put out press releases about these investigations, and none of the analysts or business writers pick them up. Yet this type of information generates business news and helps the investing public. If you have one company in mind and you're an individual investor or an analyst, you can read through all the filings for companies of interest. But if you're a business reporter, you want to find unique and significant disclosures that might not come out in a press release and might not be covered anywhere else. There are three major multinational newswires, and one of them uses our services exclusively.

If there's a significant reporting event and it occurs within the filing period of a quarter, a company can include that information in a footnote to a financial statement, or within the body of the 10-Q. If it's a significant event between quarterly reports, the company is supposed to file an 8-K with a press release. The 8-Ks are used to disclose events that could affect the stock price of the company, and this information is supposed to be disclosed to investors between quarterly reports. A lot of times, however, these events occur just as the quarterly reports are being filed. Companies hide these details in the quarterly report. Although technically it is disclosed, it's not publicly announced in mass media, and this is an important distinction. When the disclosures come on an 8-K form, it's like a red flag. Everyone looks at those, but not everyone has the ability to read through 10,000 or 8,000 10-Qs filed in a three-day-period. Through LIVEDGAR, our clients can draw out this type of information. For example, I've helped business reporters develop search strings to go through every quarterly and every annual report by every company, looking for disclosures of "unexpected losses" for that period that might not be disclosed in a press release, as well as references to anticipated events in future reporting periods.

In other examples of research, a significant number of corporate attorneys must conduct competitive intelligence, and I find information about their clients' competitors. This information is particularly useful to them for negotiating specific terms for underwriting agreements, or in a specific representation or warranty. In a merger agreement, knowing all about the competitors that they are sitting across the table from makes it possible to get what they want. They can read about what competitors have done in the past. They know when to say, "No, you've never done that before" or "You've always given this."

Another type of request has to do with keeping track of all the competitors' public filings. For companies in the retail business, one of the things you're going to do is monitor the filings by all of your public retail competitors. In the pharmaceutical business, you're going to be primarily concerned about the disclosure of product development, FDA (Food and Drug Administration) and other governmental approvals, and new testing and joint ventures.

Would you go into more detail about LIVEDGAR content, with a few examples of how it's used?

I want to underscore that the information in LIVEDGAR is from real-time current documents and not static, as are some of the traditional databases. The results are dynamic because there's a constant flow of new information, and we're able to search and draw from both new and historical materials. SEC filings come in Monday through Friday from 8 a.m. until 10 p.m. and are immediately incorporated into LIVEDGAR. The current LIVEDGAR database contains all the SEC filings that have been made and received electronically since the implementation of operational EDGAR on April 15, 1993. It also includes a listing of all filings received and released by the SEC since 1967. This part of the database provides a complete filing history for all public companies and all filings with the SEC since 1967.

We've incorporated other kinds of related content, too. For example, we just added the SEC No-Action Letters, which are not official filings. No-Action Letters are used when a company, an individual, or a governmental organization thinks it might be subject to the Securities Act of 1933, the Securities Exchange Act of 1934, or the Investment Company Act of 1940. For example, a state government that establishes a prepaid tuition program collects money and invests it. This could be construed as taking contracts forward and securitizing—that is, investing that money and getting interest and returns on it. As such, it could be considered a security under some of the federal laws, but whether it is or not is not clear. The organization—in this example, the state government—writes to the SEC to explain what it's doing. Based on the fact that it's a state, is not selling to the general public, and is taking safeguards, it believes it will not be in violation of any securities laws. Its letter is written to disclose what it is doing and to learn what the SEC's position will be. The SEC evaluates the situation and could say something like, "Based on the facts that were presented, we agree and will take no action." This is known as a No-Action Letter and is similar to an IRS Private Letter Ruling. No-Action Letters and IRS Private Letter Rulings are both forums for the government to interact with private enterprise or other parties in order to avoid missteps and violations of laws.

LIVEDGAR also offers approximately 6,000 144A Offering Circulars, which are private placement offerings. The 144A Circular is a filing exemption, meaning an exemption from having to file under the '33 Act of public registration. Instead of filing with the SEC and Publicly Registering a security, a company may use this exemption under Rule 144A and sell to qualified institutional investors or wealthy individuals. The reason companies do this is that the SEC registration process for public companies takes a long time, and this exemption makes it possible to raise capital more quickly and achieve better timing for entering the markets. It's a much faster process.

Another LIVEDGAR database is for mergers and acquisitions. It allows you to search by many different criteria on cash tender offers that have occurred in the past. Cash tender offers do not include "stock for stock" as part of their deal. For example, investment banks do evaluation analyses about the boards of directors of companies. This helps them justify the cost or the price that the shareholders are going to receive in a cash tender offer. As part of that process, they look at comparable completed transactions. They can use the specialized mergers and acquisitions database because the database editors draw a lot of information out of the SEC source documents on this subject.

A client may be looking for a company in the software industry. He wants companies with annual sales of between $300 and $800 million with, say, Credit Suisse First Boston as the financial advisor, and the buyout premium of the offer price versus the trading price of the stock before the announcement in excess of 30 percent. We can use LIVEDGAR to quickly find models that meet all of these criteria. That information is used in the client's evaluation analysis, which says something like this: "We looked at companies and deals that met these criteria. Based on that and the facts we've been given, we believe this is a fair price from a financial point of view for the shareholders of the company."

I've already described how attorneys want to become informed about the precedent of those with whom they have to negotiate. Another specific example came from an attorney who was representing a company that was going public, and they were dealing with one of the Big Five accounting firms. One of the directors of the company he was representing had been convicted of a felony in the past. The SEC rules say that you have to disclose this type of information and let investors know that a key official has been convicted and that the penalty has been served. The accounting firm that the attorney was negotiating with said that they did not now and never had represented a public company where one of the directors has been convicted of a felony. I used LIVEDGAR and found five companies that this accounting firm had represented whose directors had been convicted of felonies. This information was used during the negotiations and the attorney succeeded in convincing the accounting firm to work for his client based on this knowledge—and that was the end of the discussion.

Another example also has to do with a public offering scenario. The SEC reviews public offerings for online trading companies. In a public offering document, you must include all kinds of risk factors, basically anything that could possibly go wrong that could significantly affect the public's investment in that company. The SEC staff may write comments about anything they think should have further disclosure in particular and may tell the attorneys, for instance, that they need to further discuss and disclose the risks of computer failure and how it would affect the business of the company in question. The attorney could well say, "We don't have to because we think they have provided enough disclosure." The SEC could say, "This is the way we always do it." However, an attorney who has done his homework, in this case, by using the LIVEDGAR '33 Act Deals database, can look up all the public offerings for online trading companies, review the risk factors disclosed in these filings, and find out what already has passed regulatory muster. If the SEC has passed on another initial public offering previously, the attorneys will throw that in the face of the examiners and say, "Look, you've already done this. You're not going to treat us differently." This type of interaction is not at all uncommon.

Do the SEC examiners use the '33 Act Deals database as a way to be better prepared?

Currently, they don't use LIVEDGAR at all, but we're trying to get them to for this very reason. We've talked to a number of them without success yet. We're the authorized Fedlink [75] provider for this kind of information; it took us a year to become qualified. Fedlink is an extensive, multilevel database used by various law enforcement agencies to investigate and prepare their cases. The SEC does use Lexis and Westlaw for general questions, but they tend to rely more on the memory of the staff members around them than on databases. They're highly proficient and experienced, but, of course, our goal is to get them to use LIVEDGAR.

How do you use LIVEDGAR with regard to tracking and monitoring?

Anything that I do as a researcher on request can be set up on LIVEDGAR for monitoring based on selected parameters. This includes monitoring the filings of all companies by industry, tracking a person's name regardless of company or kind of document or attachment the name is in, or monitoring changes in tax or accounting law, which is very important to corporations and their lawyers doing compliance involving 10-Ks and 10-Qs.

Again, our clients want to see how their peers and other public companies are handling new tax laws, because they want to make sure that they're working within the confines of reasonable disclosure under new securities laws.

A particular example of monitoring involves all the new "plain English" rules. Beginning in October 1998, all public companies that filed registration statements for public offerings or securities were required to use plain English rather than legal jargon. This was new for everybody. However, we are able to provide all filings in plain English, industry by industry, or by type of security or registration, on a real-time basis, and deliver them to our clients' desktops.

How do you decide which is the right model or precedent when looking at comparable companies?

There's something to be said here about understanding who you're talking to. If you're dealing with a private law firm, certain law firms are better vanguards. The people who are drawing up these legal papers first are usually the vanguards of the industry and are respected for high-quality work and fine minds. Everyone else hops on board to see what the other guys have done and then add their own permutations.

In many instances, for new kinds of disclosure, such as the plain English example, the SEC tries to put out some guidelines. They don't do this for every new rule or every new type of disclosure, but they do have a staff legal bulletin on specific kinds of disclosure. For mutual fund companies, they'll have a letter to all mutual fund companies describing the kinds of disclosure they want, and they try to give them some guidance.

They also draw on private industry to help them create the guidelines by initially talking to these vanguard law firms and investment banks. In the merger and acquisition business, there are a half dozen firms and maybe two on top of that half-dozen that do all the vanguard work. They push the envelope on tax issues, on disclosure, and for public offerings and registrations. There are firms that just specialize in employee benefits and incorporate all the ERISA laws. ERISA stands for the Employee Retirement Income Security Act of 1974. It's the federal law that established legal guidelines for private pension plan administration and investment practices.

It's not just SEC laws that are of concern. In fact, a lot of the questions I get include the phrase "by a reputable law firm" or "by a big investment bank" or "by a Fortune 100 corporation." Clients want reputable models, not just any model, and something they can reasonably rely upon to compare with what they've drafted. In most cases, they've drafted something already, and they want to check to make sure that they're not way out of line with everyone else's interpretation of the law and how it's actually invoked in the documents.

How has the Internet affected you?

The Web has provided a lot of opportunity. Our company could not have competed with the likes of West or Lexis 10 years ago, because the key to content delivery at that time was distribution, not content. The distribution question is now erased. In general, the reliability of communications has increased as organizations have migrated from stand-alone PCs to network-based systems with wider bandwidth. Web-based usage has increased because more people have access and can get to our servers using dial-up modems or dedicated lines—from 56K lines to T-1. Internet access is becoming a reliable road from our clients' desktops to our service here. The databases that we create are nothing more than tools. What makes the research we do here special is our content expertise.

How do you stay current?

I read the current changes in securities laws and proposed rules or changes in the releases and comment letters from the SEC as a way to stay abreast of compliance issues. It's also important to read the real-world application for those laws. The laws are significant because they affect the people who use our services, and it's necessary to understand what's proposed. If a new disclosure is required for a particular regulation, it helps to have an idea of what the regulation is and what kind of disclosures you might be looking for. This is where you start for some of the research questions I've been describing.

Also, the actual research I do for clients regarding laws keeps me up to speed. I'm not a lawyer by training, but a lot of the work I do involves keeping law firms, investment banks, and corporations up to date on current law. I often talk to lawyers at their firms to gain a deeper understanding.

Are you on a mailing list or alerting service from the SEC for new laws?

The SEC doesn't have any type of notification system, but we monitor their Web site daily because that is where you'll find new electronically-released information. We also notify our clients of any pertinent changes. The SEC still releases a lot of information in paper form and sometimes exclusively, or at least a week or two before it's released electronically. We send staff to the SEC public reference room where they pick up new information. Our old motto was, "We're your eyes and ears at the SEC."

What global or macro trends have changed or increased the need for investment-related research?

Five years ago, the World Wide Web was a bunch of links from one Web site to another. Three years ago, it was a bunch of links from one list to another. Now you're starting to get real content on it. But the integrity and completeness of the content comes into question. The paradigm has changed; you'd better know what you're looking at and that it's reliable, because if you're relying on it, you're going to be in trouble if it's wrong.

For individual investors, the access to source documents is great. The commodity is there. It's more a question of education than research, and what to look for once you're there. A simple education process is necessary for understanding about what is to be disclosed from a financial standpoint.

On the other hand, I believe that quality and speed are required at an ever-quickening pace for people who really do need someone else to do their research. Every client of mine who goes from stand-alone to local network access, to the Web, to desktop access for everybody in the firm, finds that 20 percent of their employees all of a sudden become "expert World Wide Web searchers." In fact, they're not. They're wasting time and not being productive. That brings up the whole question about a greater need for more professional researchers and content evaluators than ever before. A lot of librarians are worried about the Web ruining things for them and taking away their work. Well, it's increased their work.

Attorneys, investment bankers, and vice presidents in corporations are used to getting a lot of mailings. Now, they get email solicitations about all kinds of new tools and Web sites. They're hit at every turn, and this muddles things even more. That's not to say that there's not valuable Web content that is free. But I think that the main factor in deciding whether or not it's valuable has to be the question, "What's the value of your time?" If you're an individual investor and you have time to spend on the Web, then there's no problem. If you're someone who's billing a client $400-$500 an hour, that becomes extremely expensive research that's almost unaffordable. The content might be free, but your time is not. You have to be informed, or you have to have someone who is informed to give you direction and say, "This is the information you need to rely on to do your job correctly." The need for skilled, knowledgeable researchers has to do with reliability and completeness, and with that "time versus money trade-off."

Super Searcher Power Tips and Wisdom

➤ What's most difficult before you even start a research job is to figure out what the right question is. You often find that what you've been asked is not what is really needed. Trying to learn the right question is par for the course. After that, 90 percent of the battle is done.

➤ In a merger agreement, knowing all about the competitors who are sitting across the table from you makes it possible to get what you want. You can read SEC filings that describe what your competitors have done in the past. You know when to say, "No, you've never done that before" or "You've always given this."

➤ Every client of mine who goes from stand-alone to local network access, to the Web, to desktop access for everybody in the firm, finds that 20 percent of his or her employees all of a sudden become "expert World Wide Web searchers." In fact, they're not. They're wasting time and not being productive.

Robert J. Magri
Market Data Vendor Manager

Robert J. Magri is principal in and procurer of market data vendor services for State Street Global Advisors, one of the largest investment management firms in the world. He has extensive knowledge and contacts in the market data segment of the information industry.

Bob_Magri@ssga.com

Could you tell me in a nutshell what your company does and your role there?

I'm a principal at State Street Global Advisors (SSgA) and my functional title is Market Data Vendor Manager. State Street Global Advisors is the investment management arm of State Street Corp., a public company based in Boston. We're one of the largest investment management firms in the world, actually the third largest in the United States, with over $575 billion in assets under management. Our specialty is managing pension plans, 401(k) plans, and high-net-worth individual assets, globally.

My role here has been to set up the Market Data Services Group. The definition of market data can vary depending upon whom you ask. I consider market data to be any type of information on a company, industry, economy, or market segment that is used for reference and, more importantly, investment decision-making purposes. That could be anything from real-time market quotes from stock exchanges and news from real-time sources, to fundamental financial data, to earnings estimates, company research reports, risk characteristics, economic data, and end-of-day prices. The information can come from any type of reference tool or information source, whether the Web, dial-up databases, or networked through a firm's LAN or WAN.

The bottom line is that my group is responsible for any type of information brought into the firm that is used in any part of the investment process. Essentially, there are two functional roles to what I do. One is related to the business side and the other to the technical aspects. The business side involves managing the relationships with the vendors and procuring any information that our investment professionals need. When one of the investment professional groups or managers requires some particular type of information, I will find a vendor or a group of vendors who have that information. I do a comparative analysis on various suppliers, arrange for trials for our users, and then make the purchase if the product proves to be a valuable tool. I also investigate any suggestions from the investment professionals on staff.

My clients are the investment professional user base here at State Street Global Advisors, of which there are several hundred. I make sure they have the information they need on a regular basis and in a stable environment. I create, maintain, and manage the market data services budget for both "hard dollars"—otherwise known as cash—and "soft dollar" expenditures. Soft dollars are a way of obtaining market data services that, essentially, are paid for by a third-party broker. For example, State Street Global Advisors trades a whole variety of different types of securities and equities through sell-side brokerage firms. The sell-side brokerage firms will say, "If you do X amount of business with us at X amount of cost, we will provide you with Y level of market data." A good portion of our market data services is essentially paid for through business relationships.

The amount they are willing to provide is based on something called the broker ratio. Let's say we do a million dollars' worth of commissions with a certain broker, who may say, "Because you did a million dollars worth of business with us this year, we'll pay $400,000 toward some of the market data services that you use." The broker ratio in this case would be 1.67. We get whatever market data services the broker has or market data vendors he or she has relationships with.

Most of our relationships are with major investment brokers. For us, it's usually not that tough a deal to get market data services paid for with soft dollars, because we trade a high volume of equity shares. There is an SEC rule that states that users can have soft-dollar-eligible vendor services on their desktops only if they are directly involved in the investment decision-making process. For example, we can neither buy the service and give it to a client nor use it in our non-investment-related groups. Soft-dollar market data services' must be used in the investment decision-making process.

In addition to managing the budget for market data services, I negotiate all of the new contracts and renewals with vendors and manage our vendor relationships. Getting up to speed on the vendors can sometimes be a full-time job in itself. The phone rings off the hook nonstop, with vendors calling about new products and services. Of course, I always try to get the best deal for the firm, whether it's for a product purchase for an individual group or site, or for an enterprise-wide license for a group, or even for all of our satellite offices around the world.

I also get together with users to coordinate training sessions. On the technical side, I focus primarily on providing support here in Boston rather than providing it to all our offices around the world. Apart from all of these responsibilities, we are also in the process of designing our own custom internal database for tracking our market data services administrative management data. There are several shrink-wrapped versions of the market data administrative tools in the marketplace, but we decided to build our own and customize it to our particular needs.

Do you use or conduct research on some of these tools yourself?

I do use a lot of these products on a regular basis, but mostly in a test or reference mode to make sure that I keep up to speed on the market, available products, and current products already installed throughout our user base. I don't do any *ad hoc* research for the investment professionals. As a matter of fact, here at SSgA, we don't have any specific libraries or information centers. The investment professionals are very self-sufficient, are very technically savvy, have all the products on their desktops or in common areas, and do most of their own research. I think that, as SSgA moves toward expanding its fundamental investment processes and research functions, we'll consider a different resource support structure in the future, including a centralized information manager or knowledge center. I see the advantages to that. I've worked in environments where having an information center works well.

You've used the word "fundamental" a couple of times and I know it's a jargon word. Could you define it for me?

Fundamental data basically consists of the financial statement data for a company. Balance sheet, income statement, statement of cash flow or financial ratios—any of that would be what I would term "fundamental data" for a company.

You mentioned a technical side to what you do. Could you describe that in more detail?

There are many aspects to the technical side of market data management. We install trials of new market data feeds to test the functionality and technical issues for a particular product. We usually put the product on a few of the desktops in the department that I oversee; we're six, including myself. We also ask the investment professionals who are particularly interested in a specific product or whom we think will give us the best business analysis feedback, to test it out. After we install the product trial, we put it through our stress test here, checking it for functionality and any technical compatibility or performance issues with our network environment. If it gets approved and we decide to purchase the product, we roll it out to our users in a production environment and support it on a daily basis.

For existing products, we are involved with technology upgrades on the front and back end that are almost never-ending. As soon as you finish with one, another one is waiting. We keep a lot of balls juggling in the air at the same time. In the end, the results usually wind up being what we planned for, although not without a few kinks, because Murphy's Law always seems to rear its head at the most inopportune times.

From a technological standpoint, if you set a due date for a specific project, more than likely, because of one thing or another, the deadline winds up getting pushed back. We try to build a buffer in so it doesn't get pushed back too far. Most of the time, the delay is on the vendor's end, because quite often the vendors drag their feet in putting out new versions of the product or in coordinating the ordering of networking systems, hardware, or communication lines. Much of the time we're at the mercy of the vendor. Your best bet is to keep a good relationship with the vendors; if they consider you a friend and ally, they put you on the high priority list when there's a problem. It's best for them not to think you're complaining or working against them. Of course, there are times when you have to get tough on them, but if you maintain the good working relationships and keep up on the latest industry issues and technology, you can minimize the risk of problem occurrences.

On the technology end, I have also been very busy with special projects such as Y2K compliance testing, the design and implementation of a disaster recovery site, and a major internal data center move.

I'd like to hear about your background and where you worked before you came to State Street Global Advisors.

I've been at State Street Global Advisors in my current capacity since September 1998. They did not have a fully staffed

Market Data Services Group that was dedicated to both the business and the technical side, and I was brought in to help build up and lead an entire new group. It was a great opportunity for me. On top of all the special projects going on, it's been interesting to work through the trials and tribulations of building and staffing an organization.

My previous employer was Fidelity Management Research (FMR), which is the premier arm of Fidelity Investments. This is the firm with all those investment professionals, portfolio managers, and traders that you read about on the front page of *The Wall Street Journal* every day, good or bad. I worked in a Market Data Services Group there as well. My title was Senior Market Data Analyst, which essentially can be considered a senior business analyst. I worked with the investment professional user base and was one of the main contacts for market data, as well as a main contact for the market data service vendors. In my role as a senior business analyst, I worked constantly on comparative analyses of data content, functionality, and technology for all the market data services there. On occasion, I did some *ad hoc* research for the investment professionals.

Fidelity does have libraries and information centers, as well as a few groups that directly support the investment professionals in a research-reference-reporting capacity. By default, because of our close working relationships, some users would ask me about new products coming down the pipeline or about the functionality of a product. Sometimes they would also ask me to run a report on the airlines industry or on some other technology company, because I had access to all the tools and knew what to do, and they knew I would do that for them.

On a regular basis, I assessed the existing installed products on the user desktops versus other competitors' products in the marketplace. If a user was looking for certain types of data, information, or analytical functionality, it was part of my job to go out and find it, review it, test it, and procure and purchase it. Working for FMR was quite an experience, because almost every single market data vendor out there either had Fidelity on its existing client list or at the top of its prospect list. Everybody wants Fidelity as a client because it's such a well-known name. That enabled me to come into contact and familiarize myself with most of the market data products and vendors in the marketplace. At Fidelity, I also had the opportunity to take the lead on negotiations for several major contract deals. This brought me closer to some of the vendors and also allowed me to work closely with some high-profile individuals, such as the Fidelity Chief Financial Officer.

Prior to working at Fidelity, I was the U.S. and International Equities Product Manager at OneSource Information Services [171, see Appendix A]. OneSource is now Web-based and integrates business and financial information about public and private companies and industries. I started there in a product support/help desk role. In a fairly short period, I moved into an associate product manager role, actually working for the U.S. Equities Product Manager and the International Equities Product Manager in a quality assurance analyst and project manager role. I tested each product we put out on a weekly, monthly, or quarterly basis to ensure data quality and functionality before it went to the user base. We made changes quite often and needed to make sure that none of these changes or enhancements affected any of the other pieces of the product.

After just a few months in this role and as a result of company reorganization, I found myself sole manager for the entire U.S. and International Equities product lines. As a product manager, I worked with the developers to create enhancements for my product lines—added functionality or new databases or data sources. I would find out what was needed on my products by soliciting feedback from the OneSource sales force. Also, I would go out to clients with the sales reps on a regular basis, whether to try to close a deal, prospect for new clients, or just get feedback from existing clients. I asked questions like, "What do you like about the product?" and "What don't you like about the product?" or "What would you like to see as an enhancement?" and "How do we size up against our competitors?"

Fortunately, while working at OneSource, I managed a sort of one-stop-shopping product, a super-set of a whole variety of different types of data from different vendors. OneSource is a third-party platform, a consolidator for a variety of different types of databases. I became familiar with a lot of the OneSource vendor partners. I worked with fundamental data coming through the product, as well as earnings estimates, prices, economic data, index data—and I was responsible for overseeing the analytical interface as well.

I left OneSource when it made a decision to move toward a Web-based Internet solution, because it also decided to pretty much drop the investment management client base—who are, I must say, the most support-intensive clients. With the Web product, OneSource figured it would have to drop some functionality, and money management clients require very high levels of both data and functionality. Today, I believe that the OneSource key markets are the sales forces of major corporations, corporate research firms, and management consulting firms. None of these are as reliant on the quality and the timeliness of the data as is a money management firm. My greatest interest is in the money management end and the financial data. That's why I went to Fidelity. They hired me because of my expertise with the data vendors and competitors in the marketplace. I was at OneSource for about three and a half years and at Fidelity for about a year and a half. I have been in the market data industry for more than six years now.

What's your educational background?

I went to Northeastern University in Boston and have double Bachelor's Degrees in finance and management. I haven't had time to get an M.B.A. but plan to; so far, I've either gotten a new job or a promotion or some crazy project has come down the pipeline. I'll probably try to get into an executive M.B.A. program where I can complete it in two years. Thus far in my career, I haven't needed the M.B.A. If I ever wanted to go off and start my own company or consulting firm, which I may do in the future, it would probably be a nice thing to have under my belt.

While I was at Northeastern, I did a five-year Cooperative Education Internship program. I was able to work full-time for State Street Bank, Fidelity Investments, and spend a full year as an intern at a company called Independence Investment Associates, another one of the money management firms here in Boston.

What kind of assignments did you have during those years? Were you doing research?

Yes, I did some research in State Street Bank's mutual fund area during a six-month internship. The primary information that I was using was either Quotron quote terminals or end-of-day pricing feeds from IDC [100] and Muller Data [152]. The work involved pricing out the funds and getting down to the net asset value of the fund on a daily basis. In my next internship at State Street Bank, I worked in what they call the Master Trust area for six months and was a senior liaison between the bank and a variety of their clients. At Fidelity, I worked in the trust department as a trust accountant. And for Independence, I had the benefit of working for a small firm and was able to bounce around from group to group and to work on a variety of special projects.

Let's talk about the Web. What are some of your favorite Web products or sites?

We don't use many Internet or Web-based products on a regular basis for our production-type research. We have very few Web-based products on users' desktops that we actually subscribe to and pay for as reference tools. The investment professionals do go to the Web to look at a company's Web site or for different types of investment information.

In my experience, the Internet has become a valuable information reference tool for *ad hoc* research. Very few of what we call production systems and/or investment processes are solely dependent on the Internet in order to get the job done, although I do project that it will be a much more significant research medium in the future for investment management firms. Money management is not deeply entrenched in the use of the Internet today, I think, for two reasons. The first is speed and flexibility ... or lack of it. Most Web-based products don't offer the analytical capabilities and the on-the-fly calculation speeds of the Windows-based front-end products. The second drawback is connectivity and reliability. Many firms still do not have very stable Internet connections today, and most data vendors have just started fine-tuning their Web-based access platforms, which leaves plenty of room for bugs and performance issues.

I have tested and seen a lot of Web-based versions of vendor products. Some are very good, but they tend not to have the complete data sets, and they also lack the functionality and analytical capabilities of their Windows-based, VisualBasic-based, or Excel add-in-based products.

Why do you think it's taking so long for these products to come up to speed? Companies are rolling out so-called great products on the Web that often don't perform as well as or provide the content of the original products.

First of all, I would say that the Internet itself is still in its infancy. Let's look at the investment markets as an example. When you look at the stock market, you see that many of the larger market cap stocks are Web-based companies like Amazon.com, AOL.com, or Yahoo.com—all the dot-com companies. Their stock prices are going crazy because of speculation and are not based on any significant revenue. Their P/E ratios are outrageously high. You know just by looking at this that the marketplace hasn't figured out what to do with the Internet yet. Everyone knows it's a great tool and the up-and-coming technology of the future; that's why people are investing in it. But, in my opinion, it hasn't moved much beyond a neat toy and *ad hoc* look-up service for personal use, with some business benefits.

In the next three to five years—maybe even two to five years— as companies play catch-up with the Internet, their intranet infrastructures, and Web-based product design, the Internet will become the default medium. I'm definitely not anti-Internet. I just think it has a bit further to go to become a production tool for the investment management community.

Could you define *"ad hoc"* research versus "production" research?

Ad hoc research is usually required when an investment idea comes down the pipeline. A colleague may come into the office and say, "Let's check out a particular company. I think this might be a worthwhile investment." They might go to the Web, check out some news sources, and visit the company's Web site. By *ad hoc*, I mean going out and doing quick research on a particular company or getting a particular report at any given point in time.

Production research is done on a regular basis as part of the investment process. It involves the information run on a daily basis in an investment firm's quantitative models that spit out what companies or what stocks or bonds to buy and sell. It's anything that's part of the investment process on a regular basis. Information that our investment professionals capture from Web sites, especially free Web sites, is considered part of their own work and the value-added that they give to their job, rather than as part of what our department provides.

Could you tell me about the databases you use?

Bridge Station [21], Telerate Plus [213], Reuters [188], Open Bloomberg [19], FactSet [71], Datastream [50], I/B/E/S [98], First Call [79], Barra [17], Northfield [168], and Wilshire [235] are the majors. For the nightly domestic pricing, we use IDC, and for nightly international pricing updates, we have Extel [70]. Bridge Station is for real-time stock quotes, news, analytics, and charting. It is a Windows-based product from Bridge Information Services in St. Louis, our main source for domestic equity quotes and news. We have several dedicated T-1 lines that go to the Bridge data centers. We also have another product put out by Bridge Information Services called Telerate Plus, which integrates the old Dow Jones

Telerate into the Bridge Station platform. For international equity quotes, news, and analytics, we primarily use Reuters Markets 2000 and Markets 3000. Reuters is probably the premier provider of real-time quotes and news for international equities.

We also have Open Bloomberg interspersed throughout our equity groups. Bloomberg used to have what they call a classic Bloomberg dedicated terminal, where the line would come in directly to a controller and that would go directly to a dedicated Bloomberg box. You couldn't do anything with this terminal besides get Bloomberg on it. The new Open Bloomberg has been out for a few years now and will eventually be the only one you can get. It's on the PC and a feed comes into a router and is sent to the PC on your desktop. You can do things like export the data to Excel, something you could never do with the closed system that Bloomberg used to have.

Bloomberg is best known for its fixed income information—the bond, currency, and money market tools. It also has a fairly good array of equity data. Bloomberg not only provides quotes, a news platform, and some analytics, it also offers the ability to actually execute trades. We use the Bloomberg Trade Book service to execute our fixed income trades.

We also subscribe to NewsEdge [165], an integrator for real-time news. They contract with many different providers of both real-time and periodical-type news, and integrate it into one feed that comes directly into a server that gets piped out to the desktops. We incorporate this information into a Lotus Notes environment. With NewsEdge, you pick and choose from a menu of sources and pay per service or per source. They have more than 1,000 different news sources to choose from. We use just a handful, the ones that are most important for our needs.

Have you used the .xls product from Data Downlink? Some of my colleagues are turning to it because it has financial data on pay-as-you-go pricing.

I've been in contact with the folks at Data Downlink for the .xls product [48] and I do like the way everything is exportable and downloadable to Excel. The one drawback is that, because they're so inexpensive—or perhaps the reason why they can be so inexpensive—the data sources they provide are not always the premier data sources that money management firms usually rely on. For example, they don't have Compustat [43] fundamental data, which we use here. Compustat is probably the number one U.S. fundamental data source for financial statement information. We use Compustat through a source called FactSet, and have a direct feed into some of the internal systems that we have built here. .xls is a good tool and something that we could look at as a complement to some of our existing tools, but I don't think it could replace something like FactSet, which is what I would compare it to.

Could you describe FactSet in more detail?

FactSet used to be the main competitor to my products when I was at OneSource. I also know it very well because we were big users at Fidelity. SSgA is one of its bigger clients as well. FactSet is a consolidator for one-stop market data shopping. It offers a variety of different types of data feeds in one interface. This is much like OneSource used to be. FactSet has fundamental feeds from different sources with both domestic and international company information. It includes Compustat, Market Guide [137], Value Line [223], and Worldscope [239], all key companies that produce fundamental data sets.

On the domestic pricing side, FactSet offers both IDC and Muller Data. Muller was part of Thomson Financial but was purchased by IDC/Financial Times Information. The combined entity's premier product line is end-of-day pricing and corporate actions. FactSet also offers an international pricing feed from Extel, which is also part of the IDC/Financial Times family of products. A lot of mutual fund groups use these tools for their end-of-day pricing on the funds. Or, they use these databases for historical analysis because you see the end-of-day price—and the high and the low and the volume for everything—historically. They include something like 20 or 30 years of history.

FactSet also provides economic databases, such as Standard and Poor's DRI [57] and data from the OECD (Organisation for Economic Co-operation and Development) [170], a world-wide economic and social policy think tank. FactSet includes earnings estimates from a variety of different sources. The two premier contributors are I/B/E/S (the Institutional Brokers Estimate System) and First Call. FactSet includes a whole array of other types of data sources. Its biggest strength is that it is a consolidator and integrator of such a wide variety of data. It's a very stable system. The quality of the data is excellent because, not only is it bringing in the top-notch data sets, it's also doing quality assurance testing on the vendor end. The sales and support forces are responsive and knowledgeable about the product. FactSet is very expensive, but you do get a substantial amount of value. You'll see it primarily in mid- to large-sized money management firms because of the price, which it really doesn't negotiate very much.

The interface is a neat Windows-based product that provides a lot of different analytical and graphical functionality. It has the ability to export data to Excel, which we use to crunch a lot of data in our quantitative models. We constantly extract lots of data from FactSet to load into our macros and Excel-based models. I mentioned that, for the sell-side broker consensus earning estimates, we use both I/B/E/S and First Call. On I/B/E/S Express, you get the earnings estimates, whereas on First Call's platform, which they call Research Direct, you can get the actual analysts' research reports from the various sell-side brokerage houses.

I/B/E/S is now First Call's biggest competitor for earnings estimates. The I/B/E/S parent company is Primark, a Massachusetts-based firm with several market data vendors under its umbrella. I/B/E/S is strong in terms of international earnings estimates and historical estimates, whereas First Call emphasizes the domestic U.S. estimates side. First Call was also the first to come out with analysts' research reports.

We use these estimates and research sources through third-party platforms like FactSet, but we use their own proprietary software as well. For example, we use I/B/E/S Express for current earnings estimates on a platform that allows you to manipulate and look at the data in a more savvy way than when using a platform like FactSet. In most cases, however, our users want I/B/E/S Express for quick reference or for a quick lookup. They want to find out what a particular brokerage firm like Lehman Brothers or SalomonSmithBarney has to say about a company, what their best projections are for the next several quarters and years.

In addition to FactSet, we use Disclosure [53], which is very big on SEC (Securities & Exchange Commission) [196] filings, and provides corporate reports. Datastream is similar to FactSet in that it has several different data sources, although it owns most of the data sources that it provides. It offers a very large economic data set, a very large international fundamental data set, and international pricing information. We have several desktops globally that use Datastream, although we don't have as big a user base for it as we do for FactSet.

Why do you use one or another of these systems?

We have both content and functionality reasons. FactSet has better data quality and more data sets to select from than any other system. More importantly, the interface is the easiest to use. Some users are more familiar with one or another of the products, or may prefer some of the international or economic data that Datastream provides over FactSet.

Do you use any other specialized software besides Excel for your number crunching?

We do have some data feeds that come into Sybase [211] and also into a time-series database container called Vision [225] by a company called Insyte, which is based in Newton, Massachusetts. It's a small company and our Vision implementation is still in its beta phase. It's not fully utilized in the production environment yet.

We use another big line of products for portfolio analytics, which includes portfolio risk management, portfolio optimization, and portfolio performance analysis. For these types of investment efforts, we use Barra, Northfield, and Wilshire. Barra is based in California and offers the Barra Aegis platform for global equity and risk management optimization and performance, and the Barra Cosmos product for fixed-income, risk-management optimization and performance. We get updates of data from Barra, and our users can upload their portfolio holdings and costs, and slice and dice the portfolios using both the Barra Aegis and Barra Cosmos software. Northfield has a suite of portfolio analytic tools as well. They're based here in Boston and we happen to be their largest client. We have a few installs here of the Wilshire Atlas product, which is used for our equity portfolios. There's another whole list of market data tools that we subscribe to, such as Ibbotson EnCorr [97], SAS [191], Insync [110], Morningstar [149], Salomon Yield Book [190], Moody's [146] and several others that we utilize for a variety of data and analysis needs in our investment processes.

On a personal note, how do you stay current in terms of your own interests and your field?

It's tough but definitely doable. The most important thing I do to keep up to speed and keep an edge is to maintain my vendor contacts, both the key vendor reps and their upper management teams. I do this not only with our current vendors, but also with the other vendors in the marketplace. I have them in on a regular basis to show their new products and discuss their existing ones. I also keep up with what's going on at industry trade shows and conferences. The biggest event, with more than 300 vendors dedicated to the market data industry, is the Securities Industry Association [200] Technology Management Conference and Exhibit. That's held in New York City, usually in June.

Waters Information Services [230] puts out a lot of market data-related publications. The two that I read most are *Inside*

Market Data [109] and *Trading Technology Week* [216]. Information Today [106] has a number of publications that cover the information industry. Some Web sites offer a variety of different services. Capital Institutional Services, Inc. [29] offers a good research directory and reference tools. It's actually an institutional sell-side brokerage firm and, probably because of the soft dollaring it does, it can easily provide a list and reference sources of all the different market data services it knows of. It's not absolutely comprehensive but a good starting point.

A company called Market Data Professionals, Inc. [136] provides market data consulting and something called Market Data Link, which is a good information research directory, at their Web site. It has information on all the different types of market data providers with a listing of sources and suppliers of data, industry news, reference materials, and links to other Internet sites. The Securities Industry Association has a Web site with a section called Electronic Sources that gives you a list of market data suppliers.

Waters Information Services, which I mentioned earlier, also covers market data on their Web site and describes different market data suppliers. Waters publishes two large, hardcopy books, *RTFI* and *MDI*. *RTFI* stands for *Real-Time Financial Information Index*. It's a reference guide to the content of market data services worldwide, with profiles of more than 150 real-time financial information services from 50 vendors, a couple hundred exchanges, third-party sources, and related real-time applications. *RTFI* also gives a history of how the companies got to where they are today, which is kind of neat, but it's almost a little too much information. *MDI* stands for *Market Data Industry*. Waters calls this book "the world's benchmark source of competitive business intelligence on vendor strategies, product market share, and market data user expenditures."

What do you see as major industry macro trends that will affect electronic research in the future?

It's interesting that more and more vendors are coming out of the woodwork, creating new products, and trying to find their own niches. There has also been a high level of mergers and acquisitions throughout the market data industry, which, at times, can make it difficult to negotiate a contract because there are fewer and fewer major competitors. The newer companies aren't quite as big, stable, or powerful, and can't offer you the same product level that the bigger firms do.

I can see that mergers and acquisitions in the market data marketplace are going to play a very big role in what we use and how we do our research in the future. The major vendors are acquiring a lot of the smaller companies or merging with their big competitors. They become centralized repositories and give us fewer options about where to go for data. This can be a good thing or a bad thing, depending on how it's viewed. It means a lot less competition and more barriers to entry for smaller niche players trying to come into the marketplace. But it will also mean fewer interfaces to deal with and more consolidation of data sets. As companies grow, they will have more R&D money, which will probably lead to better interfaces and better data quality. Let's hope!

There's a lot of talk in the information profession about wanting to use alternatives to the major aggregator vendors, but the new kids on the block can't always afford to give large users great deals.

That's right, and they can't provide you the one-stop shopping that you're looking for. What I've seen in the money management industry during the last couple of years is that a lot of the market data clients and firms want to consolidate the desktops into a more standard installation. They want fewer products to support and manage and worry about and pay for—as small a number as possible. They're looking for products that offer three or four different data types, or three or four types of analytical capabilities, to replace the several systems currently installed. If a user can look at two different interfaces instead of six, that's an optimal solution, as long as they're getting the same value-added functionality from a new or consolidated product set—and at the same or even reduced cost. Of course, it's always nice to see more players in the market to keep the competition alive and honest. The smaller market data vendors sometimes offer small money management firms a lower-cost alternative, too.

What other global trends are key to your field?

The other area of major importance is technology. The trend toward the Internet that we're obviously seeing now will strengthen in the next two years. I can't begin to predict what all the changes are going to be, but, on a daily basis, it's such a dynamic environment. Technology plays a major role in the success of an investment research strategy. You must keep up with technology to keep up on the edge of investment research. You must keep current on the data that's available in the marketplace, stay up to speed on the new products and functionality that are coming down the pipeline from the new and existing vendors, and, all in all, maintain a high level of knowledge on the technology end. Information and technology are two very powerful forces that enable you to acquire knowledge. If you're able to master and maintain a dynamic combination of the two, you're going to win the game and provide your company with an outstanding competitive edge in the marketplace.

Super Searcher Power Tips and Wisdom

➤ Keep a good relationship with your vendors; if they consider you a friend and ally, they put you on the high priority list when there's a problem.

➤ Very few investment processes are solely dependent on the Internet to get the job done, although it will be a much more significant research medium in the future.

➤ Web-based versions of commercial products tend not to have the complete data sets and lack the functionality and analytical capabilities of their Windows-based equivalents.

Roberta Grant
Investigative Analyst

Roberta Grant plays a unique role as professional librarian turned investigative analyst for Kroll Associates Canada, a company that serves the security interests of major corporations, investment banks, and stock exchanges. She puts her Super Searcher skills to work in assisting clients with sensitive security information.

rgrant@kroll-ogara.com

Tell me a little about what Kroll Associates does.

Kroll Associates is the world's largest investigative firm, with headquarters in New York. I work in the Toronto office. We cover all areas of corporate risk management on an international basis. Our services include advice and training on how to deal with and prepare for kidnappings, including an extensive security program and several updated online information sources, such as kidnapping risk information for various countries. We can also assist with corporate kidnappings by sending a team of people into another country. If you're sending executives to South America, for example, we can first assess the risks for sending them there and then have them met by armored cars that we supply.

We conduct pre-employment screening for banks and security guard companies, or for anyone interested in making sure that employees are absolutely honest and have never had a criminal record. I work in the Business Intelligence and Research Group, whose mandate is to conduct background checks, business intelligence research, due diligence, and assets examinations for clients who are institutional investors,

law firms, and corporations. One area of specialization is investigating individuals who list companies on the Canadian Stock
Exchanges, including the Alberta and Vancouver Stock
Exchanges. If you're a large corporation or an investment bank,
or even an individual planning to invest in a company, we'll
examine the company, the individuals, and the businesses
associated with the company. We find out anything from something as easy as the stock price—the high, low, and close—to
how heavily leveraged, financially, the chief executive officer is.

We have experienced librarians, online searchers, public record
researchers, lawyers, and private investigators on staff to handle
any kind of research in these areas. Most of our clients are corporate customers or major corporations and investment banks—in
fact, all kinds of financial institutions. We also work for law firms.
For example, I've been retained a number of times by lawyers who
want to find out about individuals who are managing companies
listed on the Vancouver or Alberta Stock Exchanges. I'm also asked
to look at the assets of various individuals.

Here in Toronto, we conduct most of our work for Canadian
companies. We refer to work for each new client as a "file." One
file that I worked on required me to research the assets of an
international family. One aspect of that file was to uncover all its
assets in Canada. The family had a listed company on the Alberta
Stock Exchange, and we followed up to find out what other companies were owned by the first company we uncovered.

In another example, one of our clients is a stock exchange. It had
some problems with a new company wanting to list on its
exchange and came to us to check out the individuals who were
proposing to list. For these types of questions, we conduct background checks and examine the companies to determine exactly
what they've been involved in, who the individuals are, whether
they have the education and credentials they say they have, or have
ever been involved in criminal proceedings.

In the United States, you can do criminal record searches to
check for this kind of information, but in Canada that's not the
case. Nevertheless, the stock exchange must find out whether

there is any risk involved in listing a particular company, whether those operating the company are honest, or whether there is potential for dishonesty that could cause investors to lose money.

When a company wants to become a public company, it must apply to one of the exchanges. In Canada, the Vancouver and Alberta Stock Exchanges are penny stock exchanges. It's amazing what's sold on these stock exchanges—like Bre-X, which was discovered to be a huge gold fraud. Supposedly, large gold finds were discovered in Indonesia and people invested their savings—hundreds of thousands of dollars, even millions of dollars. A year or two ago, it was discovered that there was no gold there, absolutely none. In fact, the gold samples had been salted with real gold found somewhere else. So, it appears that this investment was definitely a fraud—and it started on the Vancouver Stock Exchange. However, lots of people also made a bundle of money if they bought and sold Bre-X shares prior to the discovery that there was no gold in that area of Indonesia. That is the attraction of penny stock. Even if there is only a pile of dirt in the country, the hope that there is gold often sends the price of the stock skyrocketing—until the truth is discovered. In a penny stock exchange, you can invest in stocks that cost from less than $1 up to $50. If you invest in the Toronto Stock Exchange, you can purchase blue chip stocks from companies with proven positive business records, such as the Bank of Montreal or IBM, for example. The larger stock exchanges have people in-house who handle due diligence, but we've been called on to do background work for some of the smaller stock exchanges.

There have always been problems with these penny stock exchanges on the west coast of Canada. However, people have made lots of money on them and they are legitimate. There's a lot of mining exploration, which is financed in these exchanges. Gold mining and oil exploration are very high-risk investments. It's easy for people to get in and try to sell strange, trick-types of products on these exchanges. The Vancouver and Alberta Stock Exchanges are actually known to be risky for investors. We conduct what is broadly called due diligence work. We utilize online research techniques, and act like detectives who determine the potential for bad investments. We also work for some of the companies that underwrite securities for investment banks.

Let's talk about your background and how you came to do this type of work.

I've been involved in all areas of online research and have been using online databases for a number of years. I started out in news libraries right after I graduated from the University of Toronto's Graduate School of Library and Information Science in 1978. During graduate school, I worked part-time at the *Globe and Mail*, then Canada's only national newspaper. The *Globe and Mail* was one of the first Canadian publications to go online. I worked as an enhancer—the same as an indexer—one day a week, adding subject headings to the database to get consistency when searching.

After graduation, my first job was as a research librarian at the *Financial Post* for about four months. Then I worked as a librarian for ten years—five of them as Chief Librarian—at *Maclean's Magazine*. Initially, *Maclean's* was a monthly publication. When it went weekly, they hired two people to set up and maintain the library, and I was one of them. While at *Maclean's*, we were able to get the magazine onto Lexis-Nexis [127, see Appendix A], and I believe we were the first site in Canada to use Lexis-Nexis for online research.

After *Maclean's*, I worked for the *Financial Times of Canada* for three years. Then I did some executive search work for a Swiss-based company in Toronto, locating candidates for senior positions. I was there for about a year. After that, I worked in an insurance company as a research librarian for a couple of years. I've been here now for six years and, in addition to my library and research credentials, I'm also a licensed private investigator.

Could you go into more detail about the specific work you do at Kroll Associates?

I actually started out by working for the research and investigation affiliate of the forensic accounting firm Lindquist Avey

Macdonald Baskerville, prior to their acquisition by Kroll-O'Gara in 1997. The research and investigation group became Kroll Associates, Canada, and the forensic accounting group became Kroll Lindquist Avey. They needed an experienced online searcher on staff to assist in their investigative and other research. When I came, I brought my online experience and my connections with other libraries and librarians. People here were not aware of a number of online services that are used for conducting more comprehensive research.

When I started out here, I did mostly online research. I would do anything from finding the last 20 years of the consumer price index or foreign exchange rates to doing online research on an individual or a company. Basically, for whatever file came into the research group, I would go online and conduct research, consult books, do telephone interviews, and pull all the research together. I've found over six years that no file I work on is the same as another. That's what's interesting about this work. I do a lot of industry research as well, and every request is different.

Often, we will be asked to examine a company in the context of the entire industry, compare its earnings, determine how competent its management is, determine its level of initiative and innovation, and figure out where the entire industry is going and where this particular company fits into the industry. This involves a tremendous amount of online research, which is conducted in stages. I analyze the online research, along with any industry market research reports, analysts' reports, annual reports, and other information, and I begin a report. However, as I'm going through the research results, I'm also generally looking for names of people to interview about the company and the industry. Often these interviews provide really excellent, fresh information.

Frequently, our work involves conducting background research on the key individuals running a company. This background research entails research on personal assets, news articles, business affiliations, business reputation, association membership, drivers' records, and more.

Now, I'm doing less of the online research because I'm more involved in analysis. When a file comes in, a colleague and I—we work in teams in order to brainstorm—decide what has to be done. I task people here and internationally with required work, and, when their results come in, I examine, analyze, and report findings in writing or orally to our client and recommend what to do next or whether additional research is necessary.

The first part of a file is the most important part—when I am deciding how to tackle it. I usually ask other librarians on staff to conduct the online research for me first. Once I get all the information from the research department, I analyze it. Because I've had a lot of online research experience, I'm better able to direct the research process. What's especially important is that I know what should be done and what to expect. I may even suggest how to input a search strategy and sometimes request that specific terms be searched. A staff librarian will pull the KWIC (key word in context) format, or what we call "peeks," and I'll look at them and choose which articles I want to see in full text. It's less expensive to review the results in KWIC first and then request only items that seem to be relevant. Otherwise, online research can become quite expensive.

When I need research about an individual, I know that the first and last name should be input within two words of each other to account for middle names and initials, and that it's necessary to truncate names. We do have great searchers here who make it their job to know the best sources to access the most efficiently. Generally, I don't have to direct them too much, but it helps me to know how to manipulate a database to get exactly the information I'm looking for.

For one project, I was doing background checks on a number of Asian individuals, and we had to run three or four different variations of their names just to make sure that we covered all conceivable name spellings, especially since the names can be spelled differently in various newspapers. The last name is sometimes listed as the first, or the first name is input as the last, or the middle name can come first, or initials can be used instead of the full name. For example, for my name, we would search "Grant" and "Robby" or "Robbie" or "Bobby" or "Bobbie" or "Roberta." You have to search all variations because sometimes our subjects are trying to avoid having these assets found.

For researching this type of information, the Nexis ALLOWN and ALLBIZ libraries are fairly comprehensive, although not all U.S. counties are covered. Lexis-Nexis has just added a new Canadian real properties database called Canada ONPROP, which we love to use because it allows full-text searching under individual names and/or addresses. If you're doing an asset search on an individual or a company, you put in the name or run the address to find out what other properties are owned. You can also run the address of one property owner and check to see if there is a spouse. You can then run the spouse's name to determine whether properties are owned under that name only, or if there are affiliated companies under the spouse's name or any of his or her addresses.

When I conduct due diligence for investments banks, because they want to know about people they are investing in, I'll run the name in all the databases we can find. I try to uncover companies they own, whether they have other corporate affiliations, which properties they own, and how highly leveraged they are. I'm looking for anything that gives financial background. My investigations often involve issues of fraud, fraud control, or the potential for fraud. If an individual has a number of properties that are highly leveraged, I will check to see what financial condition they're in. For example, if an individual owns a house that's worth half a million dollars but the mortgage is $700,000, this is a highly leveraged situation. This could be an indicator that the individual may be in financial trouble, may be living above his or her income, or that he or she has another business that requires financing. On the other hand, if an individual who earns $50,000 a year owns a house worth half a million dollars, you have to ask how he or she can afford it and whether fraud is involved.

Let's talk more about the online vendors and databases you use.

First, we strive to be comprehensive and aware of every new information source on the market. We utilize whatever sources fit the particular file we are working on. For example, if we're doing an asset search, we certainly check for UCC (Uniform Commercial Code listings) in Lexis-Nexis. If we are doing due diligence research, we search the INCORP Library, which includes U.S. incorporation and limited partnership records from 44 states and the District of Columbia. Another source I search is "doing business as" filings, or assumed business names, registered with county clerks' offices in the 50 states. I use the Litigation Library in Lexis-Nexis, which has a MEGA file combining U.S. Federal and State case law. Pacer [173] is a system for finding current and pending litigation; it has an electronic public access service that allows users to obtain case and docket information from federal appellate, district, and bankruptcy courts, and from the U.S. Party/Case Index.

Of course, what we use depends on where the subject of the investigation or the research is located geographically. Most of the time, we start with Canadian sources. The first search will often be in the *Globe and Mail*, which is now on Dow Jones Interactive [56] back to 1977. This archive is really a bonus, since few Canadian sources include such large retrospective files. We also search Infomart [103], which has all the Southam newspapers. Southam is a Canadian publishing company that owns daily and community newspapers. Basically, it owns a newspaper in every large city of every province. Some Southam papers are also on Newscan [164], which has a broad range of text archives from leading Canadian newspapers and is especially useful because it carries the Quebec French press.

Some of the Canadian newspapers are also available on Lexis-Nexis. Another company that owns newspapers is Thomson. They own the *Globe and Mail* and the *Winnipeg Free Press*, as well as a number of other newspapers on the east and west coasts of

Canada. [*Editor's Note:* Thomson has since divested itself of most of its newspaper holdings.] If you were going to take a comprehensive look at an individual, you would run the name in Infomart and in the *Globe and Mail.* You could do an ALL search in Infomart to cover all the Southam papers at one time. Now that the *Globe and Mail* is available on Dow Jones, you can do a global search of all newspapers there. I would also run searches in the Lexis-Nexis ALLNWS library to check for U.S. affiliations or more information and clues that might turn up.

If I am looking for Canadian assets, I can check Canada Stockwatch [28], where you can run an individual's name and determine if he or she is a participant—such as an investor or a director—or a former participant in a company, and the dates of that participation. Apart from these databases, I also call around and get information such as annual reports, 10-Ks, and prospectuses. We also utilize other public records databases available directly from private companies or government sources, such as personal property registration databases, Ontario and British Columbia property and corporate registrations, and Ontario litigation information. In some provinces, this information is only available through agencies that send searchers to the courthouses or the property registrars' offices. It's really important to know what information is available in each jurisdiction and in which format. For United States information, I can access all the Lexis-Nexis databases for Uniform Commercial Codes, Secretaries of State, real property, and bankruptcy.

Could you give me some other examples of specific questions you've researched?

One of our clients is a large company that has loaned money to a prominent international family. It wanted to know more about this family and its assets. I'll mention here that most of the work I do is very discreet. If I'm looking at assets of a person or a family, generally they're not aware that they're being investigated. For this question, I was able to find assets for this family in Canada by using various online sources, although nobody knew this was even a possibility when I started out. It happened that this family had a company listed on one of the stock exchanges. I pulled the prospectuses, the annual report, and all of the corporate information on the listed company. I found that when the international family had taken over this Canadian company, they proceeded to sell all the Canadian properties and were using the company as a shell company for a large international investment.

I followed up by researching the specific international investment and found that this stock was being sold as a very risky investment. What can happen is that a listed company will change its ownership and identity. It can become an investment in Canadian or international oil exploration, or it may go from being a gold exploration company in Canada to some other type of company altogether, thus changing the complete direction of the company. This might be done as a way to get a seat on an exchange. In some cases, these companies don't want their prior identities known because of possible negative events that have occurred in the past. They are trying to get a fresh start. I think the bigger exchanges are very diligent about shell companies, and they disclose this information so investors know what's going on. But there are so many companies and so many name changes, and it can be very hard to keep track of all that.

One reason companies change names is because of legal problems and litigation. When I conduct research, I am diligent about tracking all the senior executives, who own many shares, and all the people who have come and gone. I track any litigation that they have been involved with, the ownership of properties, and the properties that have changed hands. It's really fascinating work. Sometimes you're just given an individual's name and a request to "find the assets for this individual." You find out that the subject has a company listed on either the Alberta or Vancouver Stock Exchange, but he or she also has properties in Montana or California, or all over the U.S. and in England. One simple-sounding request becomes a can of worms and the research just grows and grows.

This especially seems to be the nature of research involving Canadian western stock exchange investments. For the Alberta Stock Exchange, nothing is exactly as you see it. To get a really good picture of an individual's assets, you have to keep turning the pages backward to learn what went before. In one example, I was working for a prominent individual from Great Britain who had been asked to promote an Internet gambling company listed on a Canadian stock exchange. Of course, Internet gambling companies are growing at a rapid rate. He had started doing business with these individuals without checking them out, and he asked me to conduct an investigation because of some problems. You often hear the term "promoters" in connection with the Vancouver Stock Exchange; some of the promoters are very articulate and good at selling investment products. Our client was one of these promoters. He went ahead and marketed the Internet gambling company but was neither paid for his work nor given the shares in the company he had been promised. This brought him to me to learn more about this company. The company was in the process of being financed by a large investment company in Canada, and I found out that the individual that he'd been talking to had been banned from one of the exchanges for fraudulent activity.

If he had asked you to conduct research first, he would have been in better shape. How often do companies hire you to prevent problems, rather than after the fact?

Unfortunately, a lot of my work occurs after the fact. It's true that investment bankers and large companies are now coming to companies like ours for due diligence first, but many times I'm asked to look for assets after people have lost money. I think many people are hopeful when investing because they want to make money and they just don't want to hear bad things. In one of my first projects here at Kroll, I found out that if the individual had done a *Globe and Mail* search for five dollars, he would have learned that the individuals he was investing with had been in jail for fraud. This client had been persuaded to invest his mortgage and retirement savings. He wanted to make money. By the time I get research requests, many of my clients are seeking information about assets because they are involved in lawsuits. In fact, that's what happened with my client who promoted that Internet gambling company. He started legal proceedings after I conducted the research for him.

How do you use the Internet and what do you think about its quality and reliability?

Whenever I start working on a project, the Internet is one of the first tools I use. When doing company research, I'll check for a Web page. Of course, a company Web site only describes what the company is saying about itself. I use the Internet as one of many tools, or as a way to fill an information gap. It's something that you have to do. Also, many databases are only accessible on the Internet now, which can create a time problem if there are too many users accessing the Net at the same time. Because our work is so deadline-sensitive, I like to be able to access the same databases through the Net and through dial-up, although we are tending to use the Net more these days. We can't afford to lose even an hour on our research when our clients are waiting for results in order to make multi-million-dollar decisions.

You have to be skeptical about information from individual companies on the Internet. Of course, a librarian would trust a Web source like Martindale-Hubbell [140], the directory of attorneys and law firms, or Dow Jones on the Net. However, information provided on a company's Web site can be suspect. The way it's presented, and what information is included and excluded, can also be indicative of the validity of the Web site and the company itself.

I must judge everything that I see and usually caution our clients about any database quality issues, including the Internet. For example, for an ALLOWN search on Lexis-Nexis, I always let my clients know when certain counties are not covered for the state I am examining. The same goes for any other research. I look at all the sources critically and caution clients that not everything may be completely comprehensive or up-to-date. I follow up on all Internet information. For example, for the research on the Internet gambling company, I called the enforcement officers at the stock exchange that listed the company, and I asked questions about the individual I was researching. Because there had been a major fraud, the exchange had held disciplinary proceedings involving one of the individuals; it sent me what it had, which I passed along to the client.

Do you use any software for crunching numbers or creating your deliverables?

I use Microsoft Word and Excel to do charts. We have a whole division at our firm called VSI, which stands for Visual Strategies International. They do charts, graphs, maps, and illustrations to make statistics and information more easily comprehensible. I also create tables when I have a number of properties or companies or loans to list. It makes the information easier to understand at a glance.

A typical deliverable is a written report to our clients with an analysis of findings that includes a bulleted summary, detailed findings, and recommendations for further research or investigation. Relevant attachments are included with this report. These might be articles from the *Globe and Mail*, a Lexis-Nexis search in the newspaper libraries, or an ALLOWN or ALLBIZ search. I might attach a prospectus or a report from Canada Stockwatch, which provides information telling how the individual participated in any of the exchanges. I never make a comment about whether something is a bad investment, but I do provide information that may, for example, uncover fraud convictions or indicate that the person in question is not allowed to trade on the stock exchange for the next 10 years. The client makes the decision about whether or not he, she, or it wants to invest or continue investing with this particular subject.

How do you handle the budget issues associated with the online research tools you use?

I'm given a budget for each file and must decide how to best utilize the funds. Generally, there is a range of charges. For example, generally, we give a price range of between $2,500 and $5,000 per individual name searched in a due diligence. The cost can be anywhere within that range, depending on the complexity of the research and the amount of material we obtain through our public record searches. It also depends on whether or not we interview references of the individuals on whom we're doing the due diligence. For some of the stock exchange research projects, there is a higher range, because we find that individuals or companies involved in new listings have other companies and partners as well. As part of the due diligence process, we would want to follow up on those other entities, too, and would require the larger budget necessary to do so. When coming to a company like ours, it ultimately saves time and money to give us as much information as you can on the company or individual being investigated. I mentioned that you have to go backwards through the book, so to speak, turning the pages back to find what these people have been involved in and what investments they have had in the past. This is especially true for requests involving the penny stock-type exchanges.

The cost for database searching has gone up phenomenally. For example, at one time, the *Globe and Mail* database KWIC formats were fifty cents for an entire search, and I could run a person's name and view only the paragraph that mentioned the name. The Infomart databases are really expensive to search now, at a dollar per peek. In Lexis-Nexis, once you pay the search fee—for the transactional-based pricing model—to access a database, you can continue to modify that search without additional cost, which is actually quite cost-effective. If you find three companies or different addresses in the initial search, or you find another name associated with the first name, you use the Modify feature without paying a new search charge. Lexis-Nexis is especially cost-effective for running searches on a large number of names or companies. When searching for just one name, it's not cost-effective because of the large initial search charge.

You can use some of the other public records databases, but it's necessary to be careful with these, too. With CDB-Infotek [33], a database system containing public records, you can end up paying a large amount of money for something you didn't intend to obtain. At times, however, charges are relatively low on CDB.

Depending on what type of information I need, I choose certain databases and manipulate them for my particular purposes at that time. Our searchers spend a considerable amount of time deciding which database has the most inexpensive information; that is part of managing the file budget. For example, we sometimes search Lexis-Nexis or Newscan for Canadian newspapers instead of Dow Jones or Infomart, because we know that we can get the information more cost-effectively. However, we also find that it's becoming too expensive to search on a transactional basis, and are moving more and more toward searching with a monthly fee contract.

How do you stay current as a researcher?

It isn't easy. As an investigative researcher, I find that information from the library world is not always relevant. I'd say that I'm in groundbreaking territory, using a methodology of combining investigative methods with other, more traditional, online research. Neither profession has all of the answers. I must search out sources that are particularly useful. I'm a librarian by profession and have good friends who are librarians. I meet with my colleagues to exchange information. I read as much as I can. Often, I find that simply reading the newspaper gives me good information. I read about a Web site for a property ownership database in Calgary, Alberta. It was mentioned in a newspaper that covers that area. There are very wealthy people who have invested in the stock exchange and own companies in this region, and this type of database could prove especially useful. I attend the Association of Certified Fraud Examiners' meetings, where I learn about different investigative techniques. New sources of information are really important to me.

Can you relate a success story that involved online research?

Let me say first that, as an investigator, I'm fairly cynical. It seems to me that investment bankers want the good news: They want good investigative work, but what they would really like is information that makes them feel warm and cozy about the company they are interested in. My objective, however, is to find indications of any kind of risk whatsoever. In one case, an investment bank had hired our firm to conduct due diligence on a company to which they were about to give millions of dollars. They asked for a cursory investigation of the individuals and didn't want to even bother with newspaper articles. Generally, our clients don't dictate to us what to do, because our methodical research process entails checking all known sources for important information. Standard practice was to start by checking the *Globe and Mail* to see what had been written in the press about individuals from the company—despite the fact that the client didn't want me to do this. It turned out that an individual with the same name as an individual we were investigating had lost his accounting certification for committing fraud in a retail company. Follow-up research confirmed that this was the same individual who was going to be the president of the client's proposed investment. The client was informed and decided to go ahead with the investment anyway, but asked that this individual step down.

Our goal is to help people and companies avoid mistakes, which are often easy to make when everyone wants to make money. Another time, I was asked to check the credentials of an individual who was being hired for a senior position in a Canadian company. When I received the individual's résumé, I saw that it listed wonderful positions, but there were no dates associated with those positions, which were also with international companies. When I began doing news searches and making telephone calls, it became clear that many of those companies no longer existed, and that the individual may have been working as a consultant and, therefore, was not listed with the personnel department as an employee. My objective was to verify his employment at these companies and also to talk to someone to determine his management style. I finally found one person in England who had worked with this individual and who informed us that the individual had an arrogant management style. This, added to the fact that the candidate had deliberately provided such obscure employment information, led the client to decide to err on the side of caution and not hire him.

Unfortunately, I often find information that translates into the deal not going forward. Generally, in the corporate investigation business, if I don't find "anything," it's a happy ending for the client because it usually means that the deal goes through. I do find that clients are very intuitive. Usually, when they come to us, they have a tiny, nagging feeling of discomfort about some aspect of the deal. I would advise anyone reading this to listen to that intuition, because an investigation can mean the difference between going ahead with the deal and feeling comfortable about it, or going ahead with the deal and finding out that an expensive mistake has been made.

What are some of the qualifications you would suggest for new people entering this particular line of work?

Legal, business, or investigative backgrounds are very valuable, although experience with research in any kind of institution is also good experience. Working in news libraries is good, too. Newspapers cover every aspect of life. In one day—or even within the same hour—you can be asked for information about Yugoslavia or about a movie star. You have to think quickly; different types of questions help make you aware of all the different sources available.

Having a law library background is useful because clients are often lawyers. Recently, we had to hire a number of people as floating freelancers because we were so busy. We were looking for people who knew all the databases we use. Interestingly, we found that it was hard to find qualified searchers with a diverse enough knowledge of all the databases we use. This type of work requires intimate knowledge of many databases and the capability to move from Dialog [52] and its search strategy structure to Quicklaw [181]—the Canadian equivalent of Westlaw [232] or Lexis-Nexis—to Lexis-Nexis. You have to be able to jump from system to system without taking two hours to figure out how to use a particular database. You have to be aware of what each database system offers, in order to go in and out of them freely. Of course, now you have to know the Internet very well, too. I found that the freelancers I spoke with tended to have one area of specialty; they couldn't easily move back and forth between a wide range of databases. Legal and news librarians tend to become familiar with a wider range of databases.

For this kind of work, you have to be absolutely at ease with technology, because you use databases and different types of software to produce your reports. You can't be shy, because you spend a lot of time on the telephone interviewing people to enlist their support in obtaining information. You also need to have what we call an "investigative mindset." You have to love digging for information until the very last source is checked and the very last person is telephoned. I remember doing a search on Lexis-Nexis at 1:30 one morning, just before it closed down to update its files. I put in one last modification and found the best asset information of the whole evening's work. Your attitude has to be that you never give up until you find what you're looking for.

Of course, part of the investigative mindset is that you have to be able to spot something that doesn't ring true. For example, why does this individual live in Toronto but have his two companies in Vancouver at the other end of the country? How is he managing those companies? Are they real companies? Who is *really* managing those companies? Shouldn't we investigate those managers before we invest in the companies? It's important that a candidate for this work be both curious and tenacious. A person coming into this business should also know how to write reports, analyze the results from the searches, and present them in a written or oral way that is comprehensible to the client. Marketing is also part of the job. If you have some marketing experience and can bring in some work, that is also very valuable.

What global or macro trends have increased the need for the kind of research that you do?

They used to say in our business that when the economy is bad, we have more work to do; there's more fraud as people are laid off or companies downsize. But it seems to me that we're just as busy during good economic times as we were during bad economic times, particularly in corporate due diligence. As investments become more global, businesses may be taking more precautions prior to investing or taking over other companies. We are finding an international aspect to more and more of our files, as business people from different companies join their areas of expertise in strategic alliances and partnerships. Also, being part of an international company like Kroll means that we in Canada are seeing more work with an international component, as we are tasked by our international colleagues to handle the Canadian investigation of an international file.

In addition, the whole world is getting smaller; people locally are not only investing in Canada, but in the U.S., Asia, and Great Britain, too. If they're wise, they'll come to us first to ensure that their investment is safe. Research must cover the globe, and now it's more important than ever to use the type of research services a firm such as ours provides—to find out exactly who the individuals are who are offering an investment, because you're that much farther away from them. It's crucial to find out whether there is substance behind that investment.

The Internet is a wonderful international communication device that has made it easier to find information and communicate internationally, but it also increases opportunities for fraudulent activities to be perpetrated. As part of the Kroll-O'Gara group of companies for more than a year now, and operating in a global marketplace, it's comforting for me to have colleagues who are experts in research and investigation in 40 international locations—some as far away as Hong Kong, Brazil, Moscow, Paris, Germany, Tokyo, the Philippines, India, Australia, Singapore, and Beijing.

Super Searcher Power Tips and Wisdom

➤ Because I've had a lot of online research experience, I'm better able to direct the research process; what's especially important is that I know what should be done and what to expect.

➤ It saves time and money to give us as much information as you can on the company or individual being investigated.

➤ It's less expensive to review the results in KWIC (key word in context) first and then request only items that seem to be relevant. Otherwise, online research can become quite expensive.

Chris Carabell
Investment Manager
Researcher

Chris Carabell, Senior Vice President of Liberty Asset Management, is a senior member of the investment team responsible for managing the Liberty All-Star Funds and the Colonial Counselor Select Funds.

ccarabell@lib.com

Tell me a little about your company and what you do.

I work for Liberty Asset Management Company (LAMCO), which is part of Liberty Financial Companies, a holding company traded on the New York Stock Exchange under the symbol "L." Liberty Financial Companies, Inc. is a diversified asset accumulation and management organization with more than $62.7 billion in assets under management for more than 1.7 million investors worldwide, through an array of fixed, indexed, and variable annuities, private and institutional accounts, and 87 mutual funds. Its operating companies include Colonial Management Associates, Crabbe Huson Group, Independent Financial Marketing Group, Keyport Life Insurance Company, Liberty Asset Management Company, Liberty Funds Group, Newport Pacific Management, Progress Investment Management Company, and Stein Roe & Farnham.

LAMCO manages approximately $1.5 billion for the All-Star retail mutual funds. In addition to myself, the senior investment team includes Bill Parmentier, CEO and CIO, and Mark Haley, Vice

President of Investments. The team is responsible for designing and managing the funds that we provide to the marketplace.

LAMCO's investment management process is very different from the typical mutual fund company. Most mutual funds are run by a portfolio manager who pursues a particular investment style. This approach works well when the manager's style is in favor, but styles go in and out of favor. What produces strong returns one year may produce disappointing results the next. LAMCO relies on a multi-management approach to manage the assets in the All-Star Funds. By employing independent investment managers who practice different investment styles, we seek to reduce volatility while producing superior returns.

LAMCO'S primary role is to identify and research investment managers to manage the assets within funds. We look to hire institutional investment managers with superior performance over long periods of time. A firm may have one individual or a team that is responsible for managing the money. We primarily look for institutional investment managers, those who run money for large pensions and endowments. Our goal is to bring very institutionally-disciplined investment managers to the retail mutual fund environment. The managers we hire are typically unavailable to retail investors like you or me, since they require very high minimum dollar amounts for management.

The general concept is for smaller retail investors to put their money into a fund that is divided among several of these institutional managers, who independently manage their portions of the assets allocated to them. The Liberty All-Star Growth and Income Fund has five investment managers. They are J.P. Morgan Investment Management, Inc., Boston Partners Asset Management L.P., Oppenheimer Capital, Westwood Management Corporation, and the TCW Group. All five of these investment managers have excellent long-term track records and outstanding investment management leadership.

LAMCO is growing by adding new funds that use the multi-managed approach that I just described. As a result, I'm spending more time developing the marketing story for our investment process. I'm also spending time interacting with the various sales channels that distribute our product. To help with this activity, I use research for both product development and marketing. Basically, I study other funds with similar objectives and analyze how competitors are positioning their funds. Since we use multi-management for all our funds—that is, the outside managers that I described—our product development looks a little different than other companies'. We look at broad asset classes and our own company's fund lineup in order to identify gaps and/or unique product lines that can be filled using our institutional multi-managed investment approach.

For industry analysis, I look to see how potential competitors position their funds and what products they offer. My job primarily involves designing investment programs and finding and researching investment managers. There are two parts to my research: one that involves quantitative criteria and another that is qualitative. I use specialized databases, both online and CD-ROM, to deal with most of the quantitative criteria. The qualitative research entails a number of things, but the key variables that I consider when looking for managers are the philosophy and process that the firm uses for identifying investments.

Evaluating the key investment professionals at the firm is also a critical part of the process. On the quantitative side, we're primarily looking at the overall structure of the fund and the performance characteristics of the investment manager. We use a number of databases and modeling tools to perform our analysis. The investment manager databases list the firm's characteristics, products, people, and performance.

What type of background do you bring to your job?

The senior team at LAMCO has an institutional investment background. I started my investment career at the Boy Scouts of America, where I managed the pension and endowment plans as

Director of Investments. I then went to work for Barra RogersCasey, an institutional investment consulting firm. One of my clients happened to be Liberty Asset Management Company and, after working as a consultant to them, I joined their firm. During my whole career—it's been about 10 years now—I've designed investment programs and researched investment managers.

A lot of the qualitative criteria that we use in selecting managers comes from our knowledge of the industry, who the players are, and how to evaluate a successful firm. Each member of the senior team has an M.B.A. concentrating in finance. My specific educational background consists of an undergraduate degree in Finance and Economics from Baylor University and an M.B.A. in Finance from Southern Methodist University in Dallas. Bill Parmentier, our CEO, managed a large corporate pension plan for a Fortune 500 company before joining LAMCO.

What research tools do you use, and how do you use the Web?

One of the problems with trying to monitor some of the firms on the Web is that institutional managers are often smaller companies that don't have their own Web sites. The institutional investment management side of the business has not yet taken advantage of the Internet as well as it probably should have by now. The investment managers with a retail emphasis, like our own Liberty Funds Group, are on the Internet with extensive Web sites. But many of the managers that we're looking for are smaller, niche firms. That's why we must rely on specialized CD-ROM databases.

Let's talk about the specific databases and CD-ROMs that you use to identify investment managers. Could you describe what you use and how you use them?

We use a number of databases and analytical software packages, not only to help us narrow down the universe, but also to analyze the managers' performances and portfolios. Typically, once we narrow the universe down to managers we're interested in, we request that they give us historical portfolios, which we then analyze. A primary source for investment manager research is Plan Sponsor Network (PSN) [180, see Appendix A], an investment manager database on CD-ROM. It contains information on more than 1,450 firms and 5,500 composite portfolios, as well as performance returns for more than 8,000 mutual funds.

We also use InvestWorks [122], a Barra RogersCasey software package that has both company and product narratives. This database has information on about 1,500 investment firms and 10,000 mutual funds. We use Nelson's Directory of Investment Managers [158] with information on about 2,500 investment managers and their 9,500 investment products. They also include 400 pension fund consultants and 14,000 U.S. plan sponsors. Two other valuable sources are Russell Performance Universe [189] and Bankers Trust [16]. All of these come as CD-ROMs, with monthly updates that we get online from the Web. These products help us find managers and contain information that is useful for evaluating their performances.

All of these databases are somewhat similar, but each has a different nuance. Bankers Trust has one universe of managers, whereas Russell has another. Or, they break down their universes of managers into different categories. Bankers Trust accumulates data from the plan sponsor community, a group of pension and endowment plans; there may be multiple accounts for each manager. The various vendors get their data from different sources, too. For example, PSN receives its data directly from the managers, while Bankers Trust assembles its data from its client accounts and consultants.

Does somebody audit the performance information contained in these databases? Are there any guarantees that the information is valid?

PSN is manager-driven, but managers are held to an industry performance standard developed by the Association for Investment Management and Research (AIMR) [13]. These Performance

Presentation Standards (AIMR-PPS™) are actually reporting guidelines that investment professionals use to ensure fair representation and full disclosure of investment performance. Each investment manager is required to report his or her standards and have them audited, or to report his or her performance and have it audited. The PSN database contains managers' composites, which essentially means that all of a manager's accounts are lumped into one. The AIMR has come up with criteria for creating a composite.

Bankers Trust reports the data directly from clients' accounts via a trust department. Most of the databases categorize the investment managers by style. Domestic managers—meaning those who are U.S.-based—are categorized as large-cap, mid-cap, or small-cap managers and either growth, value, or "core" (which means "neutral") styles. They also categorize the international managers. Russell breaks its database into finer categorizations, which look at the sub-styles within value and growth.

All of these databases are geared toward investment professionals rather than individual investors in the retail environment. However, the retail data sources are getting more sophisticated. Morningstar [149] and Lipper [133] are two companies that provide data on mutual funds. Both of these companies provide online access to their databases and both categorize the funds into sub-styles.

We monitor our investment managers very closely. We want to make sure that they're doing what we hired them to do and not deviating from the style for which we hired them. We do this daily, and we know what they're buying and selling each day. Outside managers who are potential candidates for hire are monitored on a quarterly basis, whereas we monitor our existing managers for the various funds every day. In fact, I look at this information every morning. As soon as I come in, I check to see how the managers did the day before and what they bought and sold. One of the key ways to recognize deviations is by using tools like the Barra RogersCasey E-3 Model software, which we run monthly. It's a risk and performance attribution software model that we download and use online.

Basically, I use this software to monitor the managers' portfolios for style consistency.

What happens when they deviate, and how frequently might that happen?

If we've done a satisfactory job—that is, conducting our research—and we've hired a good manager and monitored his or her historical portfolios first to make sure that he or she hasn't had deviations in the past, there probably won't be deviations in the future. But if there were, we would fire anyone who deviated because we try to maintain the overall style-integrity of the fund, which is 60 percent invested with value managers and 40 percent invested with growth managers. If one of our firms were to suddenly change its style, this would throw the percentage weight of the portfolio off. As you can see, the research we do before hiring a new fund manager is really critical to making things run smoothly. We visit the portfolio manager candidates to do the qualitative part of the research. We interview the portfolio managers and research analysts, usually several times before hiring them.

I imagine that these specialized CD-ROMs and other software tools must have some hefty subscription costs attached. Can you give me an idea of what those costs are?

The Barra E-3 institutional risk and attribution software costs us $75,000 a year, which is very expensive. By the name, you can tell that this software is produced by the consulting firm I used to work for, Barra RogersCasey. RogersCasey is a consulting firm based in Darien, Connecticut, and Barra is a software company based in Berkeley, California. Barra acquired RogersCasey. The two companies combined their businesses so that Barra's quantitative research could be leveraged with RogersCasey's qualitative consulting expertise.

For analysis of retail mutual funds we have access to the databases I mentioned earlier. We use Morningstar and, in particular, one of their products called Principia Pro Professional, which is an online database and CD-ROM. We also use Lipper Analytical Services. Both Lipper and Morningstar are used to compare how our funds are doing in relation to competitors, and to analyze the characteristics of the funds we offer by looking at the universe of growth and income funds. We probably have a couple of thousand direct competitors for just this one fund. We don't track them all, but we do look at the average.

Lipper Growth and Income has two characterizations: The Index, which consists of the 30 largest growth and income funds, and the Lipper Growth and Income Average, which is an average performance of all the funds. We analyze the Index and the Average.

We use Lipper and Morningstar for pretty much the same type of information. I consider the research that we do unique, because we use institutional portfolio managers to manage the assets within the fund, and we take an institutional investment approach. Most mutual fund companies do not research outside managers. They would use Morningstar and Lipper to compare the performance of their funds to other competing products, but they don't all use the other databases that I've described. There are a few other investment managers that operate this way in the mutual fund retail environment; New England Funds and Sun America Style Select Funds are two. SEI Investment has institutional funds for financial advisors and the Frank Russell Trust Company has an institutional multi-managed program as well.

What are the benefits to operating with outside managers?

That's a great question. We do this because we think that we can provide superior performance by selecting and managing independent investment managers on an objective basis. With this process, we don't have any ties to the managers we hire. If we're good at identifying superior investment management talent, something with which we have broad experience and industry knowledge, then we can deliver a superior investment product for our retail investors. We're very aggressive in terminating underperforming managers, and we maintain a competitive fee structure with above-average performance. The closed-end fund has been in existence for 12 years and has generated a strong performance record. We're in the 20th percentile in the Lipper Open-End Growth and Income universe for the 10-year period ending March 31, 1999. Our newest fund, the All-Star Growth and Income Fund, was launched on March 1, 1999. This fund uses the same managers that manage the closed-end fund.

What global, industry, or economic trends have changed or increased the need for the research you do?

One trend is that the institutional and retail firms are converging, and there's going to be less distinction between them in the future. I believe that this will result in the smaller and larger firms doing well, with those in the middle facing increasing competitive pressure. Because we're a small firm with a unique process for managing money, we should be fine. We also benefit from being part of a larger company that has extensive distribution and marketing channels. The large firms will have the resources to create a distribution infrastructure. The cost of distributing retail investment products has become very high, so a mid-sized firm that's been primarily institutional and that is looking to get into the retail fund business is going to have a tough time.

Although we're small, we're part of a bigger distribution platform, Liberty Funds Distributors. This distribution group is made up of a number of different people and channels that distribute funds to brokers, banks, and registered investment advisors. Liberty Fund Distributors primarily operates through 60 wholesalers who are responsible for working with all the banks and brokers and keeping them up to speed not only on LAMCO products, but on all the other products within the Liberty Financial family. It's very costly to keep this type of network in place. As a result, the smaller boutique firms will have a more difficult time operating successfully in the retail fund business. If they're adding value through performance, they'll get business from the institutions.

To get back to your question, I think that additional research is going to be critical, especially for the individual investor, because of the explosion in mutual funds products and greater accessibility. There are now some 10,000 mutual funds out there. With the advent of the do-it-yourself brokerage environment and multiple-mutual-fund supermarkets—Charles Schwab, Fidelity, E*TRADE, Ameritrade, and now Merrill Lynch—I think there will be an ever-increasing need for research on mutual funds and also on investment managers. This industry is complex and changing rapidly. LAMCO researches and monitors the managers for the investor. We provide a unique and cost-effective service to individuals who don't have the time or expertise to select portfolio managers on their own.

Where do you see the investment management industry heading?

In general, I think that institutional research and management concepts are becoming more and more important in the design and management of retail mutual funds. Institutions have been paying close attention to risk in the management of their assets for many years. Individuals have traditionally been more focused on returns. Moving forward, I believe individuals will need to be more focused on balancing potential return against risks. Individuals are not only becoming more sensitive to the returns of the various investment benchmarks, but are also focusing on what kind of risk or volatility they were exposed to along the way. Institutional firms focus on building portfolios using a disciplined investment process. They manage their portfolios relative to specific benchmarks and are measured on a risk-adjusted basis. These concepts are beginning to surface in the retail-fund environment as firms seek to manage risk more intelligently.

Super Searcher Power Tips and Wisdom

➤ Research can be used for both product development and marketing. We analyze competitors' funds and the industry in general in order to provide value-added products.

➤ Institutional investment managers are often small companies that don't have their own Web sites. This industry has not yet taken advantage of the Internet as well as it probably should have by now. That's why we must rely on specialized CD-ROM databases.

Martha DiVittorio

Information Services Manager

At the time of this interview, Martha DiVittorio worked for Oliver Wyman & Company, a management consulting firm specializing in the financial services industry. She cultivated her strong financial research background while working for one of the largest investment banking firms in the world.

mdivittorio@owc.com

Let's start with a description of your company.

Oliver Wyman and Company is a management consulting firm that specializes in financial services. In fact, that's all we do. Although many of the major consulting firms have different practice areas, like chemicals or transportation, we concentrate on financial services and assist clients with corporate-level strategy issues.

Oliver Wyman has six specialist practice areas: Risk Management, Capital Markets, Retail Financial Services, Emerging Markets, Wholesale Lending, and Insurance and Investment Management. Our business relationships are with senior managers in leading commercial banks, investment banks, insurance companies, asset management companies, and other financial services firms like stock exchanges. We are worldwide and serve North America, Europe, the Asia-Pacific Rim, and emerging markets.

The company made a name particularly as a risk management modeling firm. What this means is that we counsel financial institutions on how to mitigate credit risk and market risk. Our consultants do this by building models. Our firm has the "rocket scientist" type of consultants—those who can create complex statistical models. The firm also does quite a bit of strategy work and has about 200 clients who are all top-tier financial companies. We have specific criteria regarding whom we will work for; our clients are big-name corporations.

Tell me about your background and how you entered the fast-paced financial services industry.

My undergraduate degree is in psychology. I was a humanities and arts-and-sciences kind of person, and had no idea that I would end up in library science, let alone in the financial services industry. I worked in the library during my college years and met some phenomenal librarians. After a short tenure at a psychiatric hospital, I realized that it wasn't for me and went to work for a publishing company, where I met quite a few librarians and decided to give it a whirl. I took a library science course at Pratt, fell in love with the work, and went on for my M.L.S. degree at Queens College Graduate School of Library and Information Science between 1990 and 1991.

My first job out of library school was at Credit Suisse First Boston (CS First Boston), a worldwide investment bank. I was a generalist there. It seems to me that many of the investment banking libraries are structured so that everyone does everything; in that way, librarians learn about many topics. At CS First Boston, I might be researching the meat-packing industry for somebody in equity research, and the next moment I'd be doing something strictly financial. My experience at CS First Boston gave me a tremendous wealth of research knowledge because it had a huge library with incredible resources and a wonderful staff. I really enjoyed my time there.

I came to Oliver Wyman about four years ago as a researcher and now am Manager of Information Services. I made the leap to Oliver Wyman to deepen my knowledge in the financial services sector. Here, you can't jump in quickly or just stick a toe in the water. Instead, you have to develop a real knowledge base that contributes to what the consultants are doing. The work I do is a little more in-depth than the typical investment banking researcher's work—at least that's my opinion. I see this difference not in the level of skill required, but in the nature of the client. As an information specialist, I feed the consultants both textual and numeric data that they need to make sense of a client's situation and to help build models and formulate strategies for a client's going forward in the future.

Unlike the Oliver Wyman consultants, who need more in-depth information, investment bankers want everything on a subject in 15 minutes or less. They'll bring a wheelbarrow to the library. You pile in the information and they go back to their offices to read it. They want to know everything and make the decision themselves about what information to use or not. At the investment bank, both speed and volume were extremely important. I could hand the investment banker a stack of 250 pages, out of which maybe 70 pages were really useful. That was okay, and that was what he or she wanted. On the other hand, the consultants at Oliver Wyman really get quite a bit of leverage out of the library staff. We make a lot of judgment calls and filter tremendously what we give to them. They want the answer and they want it in three pages or less. If you can sum it up in a paragraph, that's even better. They trust you, too, and they expect you to step up to the plate for them.

Would you describe your particular job responsibilities and activities?

We're a small library but have grown exponentially in the last year. We started with just two librarians serving about 100 consultants, and now are up to five librarians who serve about 250 staff members. The company has grown. Although I'm the manager, I don't perform a purely administrative role. In fact, 50 to 60 percent of my time is still spent in the trenches doing research, which is good, because that's what I love and I didn't want to give that up. My responsibilities as the manager are to keep on top of projects, anticipate the information needs of the different project teams, work with my staff to help them meet their goals related to providing data, and conduct value-added research myself. Of course, I do have administrative, collection development, staffing development, budgeting, and bill-paying responsibilities as well.

You say you have to anticipate the needs of project teams; that's very interesting and perhaps a bit outside the scope of activities for traditional librarians. How do you fulfill that role?

You have to be rather aggressive. New projects are announced within the company, but generally after the fact and usually after some activity has started. If I want to catch the project at the very beginning, I need to stay in touch with the accounting or human resources departments and ask what's going on, what's rolling off the assembly line this week. They're the first to know when the client has signed on the dotted line, even before the projects are staffed. They'll let me know what's going on, and I go straight to the project heads and interview them. I try to keep my ear to the ground to find out what new projects are sold.

When I talk to a senior person on a project, I ask him or her to describe the big picture. I'll ask what he or she intends to prove, what are the hypotheses, and what kind of data he or she thinks will be needed. This conversation also helps my users set realistic expectations about the data at the very beginning of the project, instead of being unpleasantly surprised in the middle. I find out and make decisions about the sources we don't have that I know are going to be necessary, and I begin to make purchases. I also mine our past work for "intellectual capital"—this is a knowledge management buzzword. I give the team any past projects that contain relevant information as a way to get it up to speed on the firm's thinking about a particular area that it'll be working in. I give a heads-up to the rest of the library staff by letting them know that we're going to be looking at particular topics or situations.

My outreach activities do a lot for the library in terms of public relations, because the consultants see the library as being on top of things. If I approach a director or a job manager to let him or her know that we can add value to the team right from the get-go without anyone saying anything to me first, that's a terrific marketing and promotional tool. The traditional role of librarians has been to be reactive and respond to a question that's posed, rather than proactive, which is what we're really trying to do here.

When you first learn about new projects, do you actually visit the consultant's offices or do you just telephone?

I do both, and I also send email. The nature of our consulting firm is that we're mostly a remote staff with very few people working out of the New York office, although headquarters is here. Oliver Wyman consultants typically go to the client's site. Before we had email, it was really difficult to get information to people in a timely way; there was more of a lag and a much longer turnaround time. Now, we download a lot of things from the Internet in Adobe Acrobat PDF. I can just forward these files, and users have what they need in an instant. The reports are beautiful and client-ready.

You mentioned that you purchase special resources for particular projects. How is the budget handled for these, and what kinds of items do you buy?

I think that consulting firms are a bit different from the average investment banking library. At CS First Boston, we had an embarrassment of riches. The collection was beautiful. There were resources for any question that you needed to answer. Very rarely did we have to go beyond our in-house collection. Things are different here. Consulting firms, like law firms, bill everything back to the client, including research and online time. The fixed collection is pretty much absorbed by the library budget and the company. But what this means is that our collection here is very small, really lean and mean. We only collect things that we absolutely know we're going to get value from.

You often hear that 20 percent of your reference collection answers 80 percent of your queries. We actually have managed to identify that 20 percent, and that's all we have. We don't have a lot of fat. At CS First Boston, I could open a book or use an in-house service and get the answer in five minutes. Here, we don't have the budget to buy everything. We practice "just-in-time" vs. "just-in-case" collection development. If I know that I need a source for a particular project, I will buy it and bill it back to the client. Of course, I must negotiate with the project team by letting it know the price and convincing it that it's necessary. I have to make sure that the source falls within the budget and is essential to the overall analysis and worth the expense. If the information drives the model the team is working on, it will approve it. If it's just going to be used to make a single point in a slide presentation, then we can do without it.

Tell me about some of the online sources you use.

Our primary online vendor is Dow Jones Interactive (DJI) [56, see Appendix A]. We switched to it because it is now powerful enough to support not only end users, but also information professionals. Dow Jones was a wonderful end-user tool, but the functionality wasn't there for super searchers and people who really needed to stand it on its head. They've made tremendous strides. Now all the consultants at our firm have DJI on their desktops and they're in love. They are so happy with the idea of getting what they need for themselves. Before, all information came through the library. Now, the consultants feel empowered. They can do a lot for themselves, and it frees us up to do a lot of the really sexy stuff. We're not downloading annual reports anymore because our users can do that for themselves. Of course, there's the danger that they'll assume there's nothing out there if they can't find what they're looking for and forget to let the professionals give it a whirl. But they do come to us for the more difficult questions.

We also still use Lexis-Nexis [127], which had been our primary vendor. Although there's a tremendous overlap in sources between DJI and Lexis-Nexis, some things are still unique to Lexis-Nexis. We use their public records and legal information. Other accounts we maintain are with Dialog [52], Securities Data Corp. (SDC) [199] (now a company of Thomson Financial [215]), SNL Securities [205], Multex [153], Data Downlink's .xls [48], Datastream [50], and Bloomberg [19].

What type of information does SNL Securities provide?

SNL Securities is a research and publishing company that focuses on banks, thrifts, REITs, insurance companies, and specialized financial services companies. It collects corporate, market, and financial data and offers databases, fax newsletters, and monthly and quarterly publications. We use the SNL Bank and Financial Services Datasource, which is a database of GAAP (Generally Accepted Accounting Principles) and regulatory financial information for U.S. banks. This is a subscription-based service for which you pay a single, rather hefty, annual fee and then have unlimited use of the product. We use this to get detailed financial information about particular firms or to generate lists of financial services companies based on specific criteria. For example, we can create a list of the top 50 banks ranked by assets, Tier I capital, deposits, and so on. The information is then easily exportable into Excel, where we can manipulate the data for inclusion in our analyses.

What other resources do you use, and what kinds of questions do you answer with them?

One of the most important resources our consultants require is equity research. All the major investment houses have equity research departments in which business school graduates, usually

M.B.A.s, begin to specialize in a particular field by writing reports. Equity analysts look at the performance of a company, talk about expectations for the future, and make recommendations for equity investors. For example, an analyst who follows a particular company covers how it's doing and recent earnings, as well as industry trends and where he or she thinks the company's going. The purpose of equity research is to provide investors with information about whether to buy, hold, or sell the stock. There is also fixed income research, which we don't deal with as often.

At CS First Boston, I supported the equity research function, and the analysts often asked the most complex questions. A computer industry equity analyst would want to know all about some new cutting-edge chip—who's manufacturing it, who's buying it, what new functionality it would add, and what problems there might have been with it. In short, they would want us to find information that created a picture of how this one small chip might change the entire computer landscape. Equity analysts may cover five or six different stocks in the same sector. They write these gorgeous industry reports that include market share comparisons and much more. Investext [121] and Multex are two of the major sources for equity analysts' reports.

Just to clarify, our firm is not on the buy side, and we're not using these reports for investment decisions *per se*. However, we use the analysts' recommendations to take a look at trends in an industry or identify the major players, and this information helps the consultants when advising clients. For example, investment bank clients may tell us that they are not making much money from underwriting paper and forest products issues. They may ask our firm to advise them about whether they should move in another direction. More specifically, they may want to know whether they should specialize in underwriting high-technology issues. That's when our company steps in and analyzes the industry. We look at where other investment banks are making their money, how stocks in the sector are performing, and what underwriting fees are being charged for equity issues in this industry group. The consultant will tell the client whether or not to switch to underwriting high-tech issues, or perhaps suggest that the client doesn't have enough expertise in this area and that acquiring a company that does is the right way to go.

Another type of question might involve the cost-effectiveness of migrating to an electronic environment. The answer may seem obvious, but we need to perform an in-depth analysis first. I may need to research 10 years of ATM (automated teller machine) usage, and the consultants will then analyze whether this really saved the financial institution money. The consultants would want to analyze automation trends and make recommendations about machines vs. people.

Another project might involve researching and comparing how online trading companies or those with trading room operations are doing. We might also compare a full-service brokerage firm to an online trading broker. A company such as Merrill Lynch [145], for example, provides added value with research and advice to investors; the name Merrill Lynch is known, and their systems won't go down for several hours like E*TRADE [66] does every once in a while. Based on an analysis, however, a consultant might point out that the customer is really squeezing a lot of value out of online trading systems and is willing to take the risk associated with companies like E*TRADE. If our client is the traditional type of brokerage firm, it may be asking how to compete.

The consultants also look at something called "event risk." This is when a company suffers losses due to something like fraud or a natural disaster or a technology failure. These online trading companies have taken huge hits when their systems go down, and they are vulnerable because they are Internet-based. These factors absolutely affect the bottom line. We try to help firms plan ahead for these unexpected events. I know that sounds impossible, but that's what we try to do. As a researcher, I search for commentaries, white papers, equity research reports, and statistical data that show how many day traders there are, what kind of volume online trading systems do, and any comparisons between online versus full-service brokers.

Some of this information is really difficult to get, and sometimes I must do quite a bit of phone research, not just online.

Are some investment sources better or more reliable than others?

Yes. I definitely have problems with data integrity; it's something that we're held responsible for in the library. We're not just doing a data dump and handing it over. Again and again, we run into problems with numeric sources. I need to watch the numbers in relation to trends. For example, if I notice that a stock price has been flat for two months, I begin to wonder if something is wrong. Or, if an interest rate has been fairly stable over time and suddenly jumps three points, I'm going to determine whether it's a data error or whether some event could have possibly sparked that jump. I'm mainly looking for odd patterns. Certainly, the consultants at the next level will notice something that I may not have caught and then ask me to check it again. Sometimes, I call Bloomberg to ask it about how it calculates the numbers. Bloomberg will send me the formula and I'll pass it along. That is one way to double-check on numbers.

I wouldn't say that any one source is particularly unreliable. Datastream claims to guarantee its data, and yet I've had problems with it. I've also seen situations in which companies are delisted from a stock exchange but will remain in an online database for five or six days because the system is not cleaned up immediately. This could be disastrous if I'm attempting to generate a current list of the top 50 companies ranked by market capitalization, and a dummy stock price is on the list. You can see how that could potentially skew my data. I could be in trouble for passing along faulty information.

If somebody's breathing down my neck and he or she needs the answer in 20 minutes, I always eyeball the data and, if it looks okay, I'll hand it over. But if time and budget permit, and if it's super important because it's going into a consultant's analysis and the numbers must be right, I'll check two or three different sources or make phone calls to the support desk of an online service. I speak to somebody who's intimate with the data, and I'll ask how he or she came up with a particular number.

Let's talk about how you use the Internet.

The Internet has added a big gun to my arsenal—but it's still only one gun. My main point is that not everything is on the Internet, although end users sometimes think so. I let my users know that they must be aware of who's backing the information they find on the Web. This is one of my important roles. I certainly surf the Web myself and have found a lot of incredibly valuable information, such as free equity research reports from premier houses that give it away on their Web sites or through online trading sites such as Ameritrade [8]. One site, ECINVESTOR [59] posts U.S. Bancorp Piper Jaffray [222] research about the online financial services industry at no cost. You can now get really good industry research free, whereas, in the past, you would have had to pay hundreds of dollars for it. But as I've said, not everything is on the Web. I use it as one of many tools, in addition to print sources and commercial databases.

For government statistics, like household saving rates, population, and macroeconomic indicators, I can get good information free from the Web. Some of my favorite government sites are the FDIC (Federal Deposit Insurance Corporation) [72] for historical statistics on banking; the U.S. Bureau of the Census for demographic data [218]; the Board of Governors of the Federal Reserve System for Flow of Funds Accounts data [74], and the Bureau of Economic Analysis (BEA) [22], an agency of the U.S. Department of Commerce that publishes economic indicators.

A few years ago, I would have named essential print sources that we could never keep in the library because they would disappear. Now, thankfully, many of these sources have migrated to the Internet. Many, many resources that used to be print-only now have an online companion, which makes keeping track of where the print version disappeared to less necessary. One example is tables from the ICI (Investment Company Institute) [99]

Mutual Fund Factbook. Also, as subscribers to the SIA (Securities Industry Association) [200] Factbook, we now get its tables on CD-ROM. We keep close guard over the electronic version, printing out tables as needed when the print copy disappears. Although looking statistics up in the print version of the Statistical Abstract of the United States [208] is still the easiest way to go, we now have ways around it when the book is not on the shelf, because it's on the Web.

Regarding the Internet, ease of use is something I grapple with. Time is an issue, and you've got to do a quickie cost-benefit analysis. Yes, I can get some data free on the Internet, but if it takes me an hour and a half, I'd rather go to a commercial service and dial up directly to companies like Datastream, DRI [57], Haver Analytics [94], and Bloomberg, to which we're hard-wired. We can retrieve already-calculated historical spreads between corporate bonds and money market instruments from Bloomberg, and build this information into our credit and market risk models. Through Datastream, we're able to download lengthy historical time series from which we can track the volatility of a particular stock or group of stocks. We've negotiated flat-fee, "all you can eat" contracts with Bloomberg and Datastream, whereas we download pay-per-series from services like DRI and Haver Analytics. The cost for Haver is fairly nominal—$15 for downloading what I need in 10 minutes.

My time is factored into what's billed to the client, and I must make decisions on the spot. Yes, maybe I can get it for free on the Web, but if it's going to take two hours of my time, which equals X amount of dollars, I'll log on to a commercial service as the prudent course of action.

I do a lot of high-level academic research to obtain underlying and background information. I use the Federal Reserve Web site for some of this. There's a section called Finance and Economics Discussion Series. The site has very valuable white papers written by economists on topics such as trading in credit derivatives, why investors use credit derivatives to hedge their risk, and historical bond yield spreads. It's remarkable how these academic research reports save us so much time, and they're free. I also use the Bond Market Association [20] Web site. It's a great site with a wealth of information and statistics that you can download. Some of the reports are about 10 years' worth of various types of statistical data, or Asset-Backed Market and Outlook reports. This is the kind of information we need all the time. It's difficult to get elsewhere, but it's free on the Web. Wharton [233] also has a great site with academic papers on topics of interest to us. The Bank for International Settlements (BIS) [15] has great statistics on foreign exchange trading around the world, payment systems, and capital adequacy. These sites offer really good information on subjects we're constantly dealing with.

How has the Internet changed your research style?

If a project has real budgetary constraints on database resources, and I have approval for my time but not for expensive data, the Internet opens up a whole world of possibilities. When I'm looking for company information, it's great. If I can find a company's Web site, there's often valuable and easy-to-get information that saves quite a bit of time and money, as compared to doing literature searches. Perhaps because I was around before the Internet was really prevalent, it's not the first place I turn to. I notice that some of the younger research librarians prefer to try it first. They want to see what's low-cost and easy to get, and then they'll use a commercial service later. For me, it's one of the tools I use, but not the foremost tool.

What are your deliverables and the software you use?

Our overall pattern is to search for specific nuggets of information, selecting only the most relevant articles, sections of market research, or equity research reports as part of our deliverables. I use Excel, but in the most primitive way. I'm really not producing client deliverables so much as acting as a filter and providing information to the consultants. They do the synthesis and analysis for the actual deliverables to clients.

Could you talk about the current alerting services you use?

We have automated, saved searches running constantly for certain members of the director group and on current topics that are "hot." Since we've rolled out Dow Jones at the desktop, each individual can set up his or her own monitoring services. In fact, this is one of the most heavily used features of the Dow Jones service by end users. We also have a clerk who manually goes through the *Financial Times, The Wall Street Journal*, and *American Banker* each week looking for news about our clients. He writes up brief synopses of the articles and disseminates these throughout the firm.

How do you stay current?

I read *EContent* [62], *ONLINE* [172], and *Information Today* [106]. If something on the cover of *Searcher* [194] grabs me, I'll read it. The most important activity is a constant dialogue with my colleagues. Through the Special Libraries Association (SLA) [206], I come into contact with professional colleagues and we talk about issues, stumpers, and new products. I've also been active in the Business and Finance Chapter of SLA here in New York. You have to be fairly proactive; nobody's going to come to you and tell you all these things. You've got to call others and ask for help, ask whether they have encountered a particular situation before. It's remarkable what you can get out of an exchange of ideas like that. I'm happy to do it for others when they call me. To stay current on industry products and issues, I attend the Securities Industry Association Convention, which features a trade show with exhibits, and I attend the National Online Meeting [156] in New York every year.

Tell me about success or horror stories that involve investment research experiences.

Data reliability and quality gaps are frustrating problems that have caused a certain amount of distress. I'm thankful that the successes far outnumber the horror stories. The consultants and directors comment positively on the services I provide. In fact, jobs are often sold on the strength of the information from the library. This is difficult to quantify, but the consultants keep coming back and sometimes say that we in the library can work miracles.

What are your recommendations for researchers just starting out?

Don't attempt to master the entire Web or rely on it too heavily. Because there is so much information, it's important to realize that nobody can really be a Web "expert." Remember that commercial services often have considerable added value—such as search functionality, ease of use, and quality control.

Super Searcher Power Tips and Wisdom

➤   To anticipate the needs of project teams, you have to be rather aggressive and keep an ear to the ground to find out what new projects are being sold. Talk to the project manager and ask for a description of the big picture.

➤   Here, we don't have the budget to buy everything. We practice "just-in-time" vs. "just-in-case" collection development.

➤   If a request is super-important because the information is going into a consultant's analysis and the numbers must be right, I'll check two or three different sources, or make phone calls to the vendors' support desks to find out how the figures are derived.

Nathan Rosen
Corporate Law Librarian

Nathan Rosen is an attorney, corporate law librarian, intranet developer, author, researcher, and dad. He is Vice President of the Legal and Compliance Department of Credit Suisse First Boston, where he responds to complex business, investment research, and due diligence questions for one of the world's largest global investment banking firms.

nathan.rosen@csfb.com

How did you get started on the path to becoming a librarian for an investment banking firm?

My key role model was my mother, Golda Rosen. She first exposed me to the wonderful world of libraries, as she was responsible for our synagogue's library when I was very young. The most important characteristic she taught me was service. She was a social worker who, all her life, was dedicated to helping people—it permeated her very existence. Her example has helped me to remember to keep my focus on service, and ultimately, that focus will be why librarians have a place in the future of information.

You work for one of the world's largest financial services companies. Could you tell me what your company does and what kinds of clients you serve?

It's probably easier for me to read you a few lines from our annual report:

"Credit Suisse First Boston (CSFB) is one of the largest banking institutions in the world, with total consolidated assets of approximately $278 billion. As a leading global investment bank, the Bank provides a wide range of financial services from locations around the globe to corporate, institutional, and public-sector clients and high-net-worth individuals worldwide; and engages in investment banking, equity, fixed income, and derivatives and private equity investment businesses on a worldwide basis. The Bank employed approximately 17,200 people as of December 31, 1999. The company has four core businesses: fixed income and derivatives, equity, investment banking, and private equity. 1999 revenue and net income reached records of $9.8 billion and $1.26 billion, respectively."

I've heard your company referred to as First Boston and as Credit Suisse. What is the correct name?

There have been various mergers. Currently, Credit Suisse First Boston (CSFB), where I work, is one of six business units of the Credit Suisse Group. The other groups are Credit Suisse, the retail bank; Credit Suisse Private Banking, which mostly serves private investors in Switzerland; Credit Suisse Asset Management, which is for institutional and mutual fund investors worldwide; an insurance company called Winterthur Group; and Personal Financial Services Europe.

Tell me about your current job and your background, and how you became involved in investment-related research.

I was hired to set up a top-quality information service for the Legal and Compliance Department at Credit Suisse First Boston in New York City several years ago. The importance of information to the Legal and Compliance Department can be illustrated by the fact that one of the first acts of the then-General Counsel for the Americas (now Executive Vice President for Legal and

Regulatory Affairs) was to decide that the department needed a substantial modern legal library.

The Legal and Compliance Department serves the entire firm. Because I'm physically located in the midst of the attorneys and closely integrated into the legal department, I'm often of service right from the very start of a project, sometimes as the attorneys are still on the telephone or at the first sign of a new matter or issue.

I created the law library from scratch, putting in racks for periodicals and developing a book collection. As an important part of the collection, we've loaded some CD-ROMs onto a computer network. I also provide online services to the entire legal staff. The library can be used for training, orientations, and product demonstrations, and is also conducive to quiet and privacy. Some of the attorneys use it to draft papers or to hold a quick meeting.

Prior to coming here, I was the Library Director at the Association of the Bar of the City of New York, and for 12 years was Associate Library Director at Proskauer Rose LLP, a large, New York City-based law firm. I also worked part-time or on special projects for more than 10 years in public, university, law school, and private company libraries, as well as having practiced law for over four years.

While in library school, I worked for the business library of Shearson Lehman Brothers in the investment banking area and did consulting jobs for Morgan Stanley's business library and the Ford Foundation's library. I have a Master of Science degree from Columbia University School of Library Service (1984), and a Juris Doctor from the University of Missouri at Kansas City School of Law (1979).

What are your job responsibilities at Credit Suisse First Boston?

It's my good fortune to be working with a knowledgeable and talented team. I'm available to the Credit Suisse First Boston Legal and Compliance Department staff and to the entire company regarding certain legal or investigative research. Although it was not initially part of my job description, I established a comprehensive intranet for the Legal and Compliance Department as an alternative to reaching me, since I can't be here 24 hours a day, 7 days a week, and the library is a one-person library.

The intranet has links to stock markets, securities organizations, stock prices, public company information, and other companies' Web sites that deal with securities. I've loaded documentation about using various online services and CD-ROMs to assist staff when I'm not here. An online Library Guide serves as a basic description for all the library services; it includes hypertext links to a wide variety of forms, such as routing, office copies, and reference requests.

Let me ask you a more specific question about your job responsibilities. You said that you provide legal and investigative research. Could you explain more about what that consists of and what types of questions you're asked?

As an example of one question that's a good reflection of business investment research, I was asked for information about "green" or environmentally sound kinds of investments. I found this to be a very interesting project that was relatively straightforward to answer. It turned out that the Credit Suisse Group had been one of the first providers of investment funds with an ecological and ethical focus in Europe. I found that the World Bank [238, see Appendix A] and some nonprofit institutes and organizations have really made an effort to collect information about environmentally sound or public-spirited companies, and I was able to answer the question quickly and completely using online information.

What sources did you use for this project?

First, I tried Lexis-Nexis [127]. This is because the firm's Business Library had negotiated a very good contract that provides us with highly competitive pricing. Many librarians, myself included, often find the Lexis-Nexis News files to be a great first step for coverage of mainstream magazines and newspapers, newsletters, news reports, radio shows relating to news, and television transcripts. I started there and came up with names of a few key companies, organizations, and individuals. Other times I might start with Westlaw's [232] Newspaper, Magazine and News Services group of files, which include more than 3,000 publications from Dow Jones Interactive [56].

After the Lexis-Nexis search, I went to the Internet to look up the organizations I had identified during the news search. I knew that these strong, nonprofit agencies would be likely to have Web sites. I found quite a number of organizations focused on green or "appropriate" investing. These sites, in turn, sent me to places within the World Bank and the International Monetary Fund [114], and to a United Nations [217] group that was looking at appropriate investing from the point of view of helping people, saving lives, and advancing Third World countries and bringing them into the modern age.

The Internet gave me a lot of good information, very focused and, of course, somewhat biased—but you go in knowing that. Then I went back and started picking up annual reports and gathering statistics from different articles to expand on the variety of information I wanted to provide. In this case, some of the annual reports came directly from the company Web sites, but I also used Disclosure Global Access [53], and our firm keeps a collection of annual reports in paper, the glossy kind, which we sometimes get directly from companies we're interested in.

Could you describe some other projects?

Another interesting project had to do with women's investments. Just as people are sensitive to the growing need for environmentally sound investments, there is a whole area of investing related to women investors. For this project, again, I went to the News library on Lexis-Nexis and found some discussions of women as evolving investors, how they are more in control of their own economics now because of more education and opportunities in the workplace, and that they are more confident and self-reliant.

I found a number of very important women's investment Web sites. There are places like iVillage [124], a woman's online network with a lot of information about investing when you click on MoneyLife. Another site that's easy to remember is the Women's Institute for Financial Education [236], since its acronym is WIFE. One of the most interesting names was Cassandra's Revenge [31]. It's actually geared to the serious beginner. It doesn't provide financial calculators or stock tables, but it does have many interesting articles related to everything from initial public offerings to planning for retirement. Another is Women's Wire [237]. There are others, but these are a few that I thought were particularly interesting.

Many of my routine research requests aren't strictly about investment-related issues but are more general, or business-oriented. I might get a question about foreign exchange rates. One of my users was trying to figure out how to calculate a certain value, and I was asked to provide the foreign exchange rates. I also provided an historical analysis for the time period of interest, about two months. During that two-month period, the exchange rate changed substantially—two or three times. I used Dow Jones to find currency rates, pulled that information into an Excel spreadsheet, and created a column for calculation. Not only did I wind up providing a list of exchange rates, day by day, but I also calculated the change as a percentage of the current rate through the use of Excel. I did a Lexis-Nexis News search, too, to try to find explanations that would help us understand what was going on, and I wrote a synopsis for each of the big changes and a summary about precipitating causes for the change. This type of information was used to decide on correct rates for settling the question.

You mentioned that you had worked at the Shearson Lehman Brothers business library. What tools did you use for research at that time?

One of the best sources I learned about a long time ago was actually a wonderful print tool called F&S Index, which is also on

Dialog [52], now as the Gale Group F&S Index, File 18 [86]. The print version was nice because it allowed you to get a quick overview of what was going on in a company, as well as whether there were a lot of articles or just a few on your topic. The F&S Index was organized in many different ways, for instance, by SIC code, and by event and activity codes that allowed you to really drill down into a topic or area. If you were looking for all the airline mergers involving companies larger than a certain size, you could quickly find just what you needed by using the event, activity, and SIC codes.

Many people neglect to consider using the printed manual, which is available from the vendor. The manual, which is also used for searching the PROMT [178] database, has numerical codes as well as product terms. It's somewhat complicated to use, but allows you to create very precise searches. You can get the information online, too, but I think it's because I started using it in print first that I know how valuable the codes can be for setting up a search before jumping online.

What kinds of questions would you be jumping online to answer, for instance?

People would rush up to me and say, "I've got to know all about a company," or they wanted to know what was going on in this or that industry, or who the leading player is and if he or she is open for a change in corporate control. I would start off by doing some background checking on the company, and often would begin with a Dun & Bradstreet [58] credit report because that often gives you some good background, including information about finances. If a company was public, I'd get the financial statement from the SEC [196] collection. This was many years ago, and at that time, Shearson Lehman Brothers had a tremendous microform collection of SEC documents and a couple of people who spent all day long standing at very large, very quick copy machines that took microform and printed out the SEC reports.

For public companies, it's always necessary to look at the SEC filings. After that, it's important to do all kinds of searching, from looking at books that describe corporate histories to using Web sites in today's research environment. I'd look at company databases on Dialog or Dow Jones. Nowadays, there are other sources, like Bloomberg [19], which didn't exist during my earlier years in the field.

Tell me about your research related to building and maintaining the CSFB intranet.

To build and maintain an intranet, it's helpful to first read a wide variety of professional journals that have useful information, such as *Internet Newsletter* [116], *InternetWeek* [117], *Internet World* [119], *EContent* [62], *ONLINE* [172], *Searcher* [194], *Internet Lawyer* [115], *Informed Librarian* [107], *Information Outlook* [105], and *Information Today* [106]. It's important to subscribe to all kinds of electronic discussion groups, review the continuous pile of literature that comes in the mail, and go to conventions to learn about everything that's new.

When I find something particularly relevant to my department or to potential research questions from my patrons, I load the information onto the intranet. The idea is that, instead of 140 or so people maintaining huge sets of bookmarks that go out of date and change all the time, I keep the most important resources on the intranet. Everybody has a set of bookmarks unique to him or her, but I try to put on the intranet anything that might be useful across the board. This includes everything from links to search engines, to the best places to go within federal, state, or local government agencies for certain types of information, or how to locate attorneys. I include sites such as all the stock markets that we are involved in or sit on, and the SROs (self-regulating organizations), such as the New York Stock Exchange [162], Philadelphia Stock Exchange [174], National Securities Clearing Corp. (NSCC) [157], and NASD (National Association of Securities Dealers) [155]. For some of these organizations, we have printed material, too, but sometimes there's nothing as good as going online. Some of the organizations are so important that we've loaded CD-ROMs devoted to them onto the company network, which I mentioned earlier. But you also want to be able to access their Web sites quickly through links for the most current information.

I have also set up a section called Important Securities Sites, which consists of URLs for organizations or law firms that focus on securities, such as Morgan Lewis [147], McDermott Will & Emery [141] and Ballard Spahr [14]. These sites all provide securities law material, reports, and other resources for researching securities issues. They flag new development and, in a few paragraphs, explain the implications of these developments.

Another one of the Important Securities Sites is the Stanford Securities Class Action Clearinghouse Center [198] from the Robert Crown Law Library at Stanford Law School. This site collects complaints, orders, and articles about class actions against companies. I use this resource myself when we get inquiries that require me to identify class action suits. I will research this site and find out that there is, in fact, a class action suit in process, even if searching other online databases does not reveal its existence.

Another good site is the Center for Corporate Law at the University of Cincinnati College of Law [219], which contains primary material on securities law. Our departmental intranet also has links to the more standard sources of business and company information, such as the Wall Street Research Network (WSRN) [228], CNNFinancial [37], Stock Point [209], and Quote.com [182]. All of these are good sites, although not as heavily used as in the past. Many of the staff are now using ADP [1] and Bloomberg since they are readily available on everybody's desktop. Instead of going to the Internet for stock quotes, stock charts, or company information, they get what they want from ADP or Bloomberg— or touch base with the CSFB's Business Library. We have a marvelous Business Library in the New York office with a dedicated staff of experienced professionals and very skilled top management under the direction of Pamela Rollo. They assist in providing information in so many formats and so transparently and invisibly, without extra cost to the attorneys, that the legal staff often doesn't feel the need to use the Internet at all, despite the fact that it's a great tool for some basic information.

Could you talk a little more about ADP and Bloomberg? What information do these companies supply?

This is another example of constant change. Both ADP and Bloomberg are key online services that have historically played a significant role in research for the investment area. Both services are changing and improving. ADP provides real-time news from some 70 news sources, market data from over 100 stock exchanges, and research and analytic services, including quotations and monitoring services. This is a desktop application; the individual attorneys use ADP from their own computers. We pay for it based upon the number of users. There are different formats, and you can decide how to display different pieces of ADP at any one time. The investment banking people have one format and the equity people have another. The common configuration for those in Legal is to set the top part of the screen with rolling news headlines. They can see whatever is coming across the wire in real time.

For Bloomberg News, also in real time, you choose a menu, select "News" and a category, and you get the news on your screen. It rolls up or down as news stories come out. Both ADP and Bloomberg provide market quotes. On the bottom part of the screen, you can identify a stock you're interested in or that the firm is interested in. Since the information is in real time, stock prices are constantly updated as changes occur.

What other databases and reference tools do you use, besides the ones you've mentioned?

I'm generally responsible for our contracts with Westlaw, Compliance International [42], Commerce Clearing House [39], Lexis-Nexis, ADP, and Bloomberg. The staff also uses the Credit

Suisse First Boston's Global Research Library, which is a tremendous and extremely valuable internal collection of company and industry research reports produced by our analysts and economists. As liaison to the CSFB Business Library, I often assist Legal and Compliance Department staff in conducting business and investment research using tools and sources that I am familiar with, having used them for many years. Some of these are Dun & Bradstreet Credit Reports, Dialog, Dow Jones, the Research Bank Web [187], ProQuest [179], Moody's [146], Standard & Poor's [207], Value Line [223], Datamonitor [49], CorpTech [45], CDA/Spectrum [32], and SEC documents via Disclosure CD-ROM [53], SEC EDGAR [196], LIVEDGAR [134], Federal Filings [73], or printed annual reports.

We subscribe to CD-ROMs from two vendors, Compliance International and Commerce Clearing House (CCH). Compliance International produces Books on Screen. It is a database of rules and regulations for the securities and banking industry, and an excellent tool for our legal and compliance professionals. The CD-ROM is updated biweekly and the Web site is updated on a daily basis.

The Federal Securities Law Reports CD-ROM from CCH includes the entire content of the multi-volume loose-leaf reporter. The loose-leaf is one of the key sources for the lawyers at Credit Suisse First Boston, and it is the standard in the entire securities industry. It can be used as a book, accessed via its index, or searched using either keywords or citations. The CD-ROM has become a favorite of many of the attorneys because it is always on the shelf, always filed correctly, and provides more access points than the printed source. The purchase of the CD-ROM has allowed me to reduce expenditures for the library by eliminating print subscriptions and reducing the amount we have to pay to file the weekly updates. CCH also offers access to the source on the Internet, and some of the CCH services are available on either Lexis-Nexis or Westlaw.

We have the NASD and the New York Stock Exchange searchable CD-ROMs also, including their rules, constitution, guidelines, information memos, interpretative releases, and anything else they send out. These are easier to use than the counterpart Web sites. The CD-ROMs contain information that, until recently, was not available on either Lexis-Nexis or Westlaw. Updates are every three or four weeks, which means there's always a lag time. That is one reason for having to go online to the Web versions at times.

You've mentioned using many sources for SEC filings—printed annual reports, Disclosure, EDGAR from the SEC, LIVEDGAR, Federal Filings, and so on. What is the purpose of having so many versions or approaches to basically the same documents?

Sometimes we need glossy versions of annual reports because they're much nicer to use. You may want to examine the pictures or the quality of the report, or you may need to see the colors in charts. Even though images are available in some of the online databases, you may still want to order the physical documents to keep on file.

As to why we access so many different electronic versions of SEC filings, which system we use often depends on its presentation. Sometimes you want just a simple list of filings and you use one service for that type of output. On the other hand, sometimes you want to quickly summarize the annual report. One of the nice things about LIVEDGAR is that it organizes all the different filings in pieces and gives a more visual presentation with hypertext links.

Sometimes, we use Federal Filings to get documents that are not online. Not all SEC documents are available online from EDGAR, LIVEDGAR, or others. You still have to get certain filings on paper. Other times, the patron may want to download financials into a spreadsheet to perform a comparison or calculations, and one system or another is better for this.

What software do you use for crunching numbers or creating deliverables?

I use Excel heavily for a wide variety of tasks—everything from keeping reference and interlibrary loan logs to Continuing Legal Education (CLE) attendance records, and for budget and subscription records. I sometimes use Excel rather than Microsoft Access for minor database functions, because of the ease of use and its widespread accessibility throughout the office.

In what form do you deliver research results?

About one-half of all research is provided to the patron only in electronic form, either by email attachments, files on shared network drives, or through our intranet. Most of the other half consists of printouts. A few people want an executive summary or conclusion.

How much time do you spend on research and how much on formatting or massaging the output?

Most of my time is actually spent on research. Only a small portion of the requests I work on require further refinement or analysis. For some of those, I prepare PowerPoint presentations. I spent some time creating a deliverable for that project I mentioned on foreign exchange rates. After finding the information, I did statistical analysis on the data using Excel, as well as preparing a narrative report about the reasons for the various changes on certain days.

We've already talked quite a bit about Internet resources. In what other ways do you use the Web, electronic discussion groups, or email?

Both the Legal and Compliance staff and I use the Internet every day for all types of business and legal research. Some of the sources I haven't mentioned are TheStreet.com [214] and Finance.Yahoo.com [241], which have a good collection of links to other sites that you might wish to go to. Government sites, like the Federal Reserve [74], the Securities and Exchange Commission, and the New York State Banking Department [161] are always important in our area of practice.

As part of my job responsibilities, I subscribe—in digest form whenever possible—to nearly 50 electronic discussion groups in areas like law, technology, the Internet, and electronic business, and I receive some 30 daily email news digests or newsletters. I screen, filter, and redistribute email about companies, organizations, and the stock exchanges to the attorneys as appropriate. I have set up some of this email to forward automatically; others I review manually and distribute selectively.

How do you manage to keep up with so many discussion groups?

There are days I'm not sure I do keep up. When I am away from the office, I sometimes suspend some discussion groups, but I often use my laptop to keep up when I'm at conventions and even on vacation. There's no easy answer; you just have to keep plugging through. I belong to so many groups because I'm insatiably curious about what people have to say. I find that, no matter how well positioned I am or how many information and people resources I have access to, I never know enough about what's going on in the world. In the library profession and in business, you have to make a constant effort to stretch and to see what other people are saying.

My mother used to say to me, "If you're not growing, you're dying." The same thing is true about researching and keeping on top of what's going on. If you're not spending time tracking down all the news and latest changes, then you probably are losing track in your profession, because you're no longer as current or as on top of the changes that are important to you, day to day.

Do you use any other alerting services for your staff or for yourself?

I have recently been using a very good news summary service called Newscan [164], on technology topics. One popular current alerting service among librarians is Edupage [64]. When you sign up for *The New York Times on the Web* [163], which is free, you can set up a current awareness search. If you're interested in the business section, you can have them send *The New York Times Summary of Business*, which is a Web-browsable page delivered in email. If you're interested in more information, you click and get the full-text story.

What about non-online ways to stay current and maintain an edge?

I regularly read the key print newspapers—*The New York Times, The Wall Street Journal* [226], *American Banker* [4], *New York Law Journal* [160], and *Financial Times* [77]. I also subscribe to more than two dozen weekly print journals, and more than 40 biweekly and monthly print publications such as *EContent, ONLINE, Searcher, Information Today*, and *Informed Librarian*.

I religiously attend educational programs offered by my local chapters of the major library and information science organizations, and attend conventions and conferences sponsored by other relevant organizations. I also listen to people talking; I listen to something my daughters repeat from one of their favorite characters, Ms. Frizzle from the Magic School Bus: "Take chances, make mistakes, get dirty."

The key is to be willing to try new things, make mistakes, and learn. I firmly believe that life is a continual learning opportunity, and it is up to all of us to take full advantage of the wide variety of different things that can be learned.

I know that your expertise as an electronic researcher is reflected in your many articles. Do you find yourself doing a lot of research for yourself?

Yes, absolutely. I'm like all librarians. The first step for any good writing is research. While I may know a lot about a lot of topics, and think I know everything in some cases, I never really do until I research it. All good librarians usually do at least some amount of cursory research before they write. I start by using my own personal subject file. I've kept it over many years. It has hundreds of folders with all the trends and topics that I'm particularly interested in. I also do an online search, and usually I'll call at least one or two people whom I know are particularly interested in the topic, and share a few ideas before I actually begin writing. Many times, I will actually submit a copy of my article to one or more persons to bounce it off them prior to sending it in for publication. I always find that some level of collaboration substantially improves the end product. The more people, and the more eyes and insights that go into something, the better the product will be, as compared to just writing off the top of my head.

Earlier, you mentioned both Lexis-Nexis and Westlaw. Do you use one or the other more?

I use and love both products. They are wonderful. It's hard to imagine today's lawyer practicing law without online research. The competition between the two vendors for the online market is a hotly-fought battle and has benefited the legal community and contributed to improving both products. I am friendly with and have a long history with both Lexis-Nexis and Westlaw, having used both services since 1978. I have used both services regularly, meaning daily, over the last 15 years. I've been involved in negotiating contracts with both companies.

Having said that, I'll say that, at any specific time, one company may provide more comprehensive or more cost-effective services in a given area or topic. This has changed dynamically, by which I mean that what was true six months ago may not be true today, and may not be true six months from now. A lot depends on the individual contract you've negotiated and on usage patterns.

Regarding research, both Lexis-Nexis and Westlaw offer extensive public records databases, but they are still in the process of developing comprehensive public records files useful to investment research. Sometimes, a patron comes in with the name of a company or a property and wants to know who owns it and if there are any legal filings. The first place to go is to various public records to find the real estate ownership records, any real estate transfers, liens, judgments, bankruptcy filings, or Secretary of State filings.

An extremely competitive area is that of providing information about court dockets. I'm always looking up court docket information to see whether somebody is being sued. Online access to court docket information started only a few years ago with PACER (Public Access to Court Electronics Records) [173]. Public access then increased substantially because of the introduction of CourtLink [47] , which made PACER more useable by developing a software front end that allowed the user to access PACER information more easily. After a while, Courtlink became available as a gateway database on Westlaw.

Now, two additional vendors have Internet-based systems that can be used to monitor and retrieve dockets for most federal district courts and for finding cases involving issues, clients, competitors, law firms, and judges. In addition to CourtLink, the key competitors are MarketSpan [139], which produces CaseStream, and RIS Legal Services, which produces CourtExpress [46]. What's available in this area changes constantly; it's almost impossible to be sure that one knows what's going on. You have to spend a lot of time keeping up.

You've talked about vendors who supply public records. Could you explain more about how this type of information fits into the world of investment research?

Public records information is necessary before, during, and after companies are involved in transactions with each other. Sometimes, lawyers are brought in ahead of a project and need due diligence work done before deciding what to do and what to recommend. Often, they are looking for potential changes with regard to the economics of a deal, and they need information that will help them write a new clause. They don't want to kill the deal but, based on the information they find, may need to make modifications.

An example of the need for public records information might be in the rebundling of a note or "serializing," such as putting together a series of real estate purchases and then selling interest in the entire lot. The concept of a REIT, or real estate investment trust, is to take many mortgages, pool them, and sell the pieces of the pool instead of selling one mortgage alone, since one doesn't know whether any individual mortgage might default. Because there are many mortgages in a REIT, one can make a statistical judgment on how much the investment will return. REITs are securities and can be sold just as you would sell any other stock or bond. Some banks may not want to hold onto real estate because it ties up their capital, plus the chance that a borrower will default. The bank sells mortgages or a group of mortgages to a reseller who, by holding a lot of them, reduces the chance of default—and funnels money back to the bank for reinvestment on other mortgages.

There are examples of this type of transaction in the entertainment industry. A performer's future revenue stream may be sold as an investment. The entertainer reaps the benefit by getting money now, based upon future possible earnings. Investors may own a small percentage of revenue streams that will come from future royalties. This is a pretty interesting concept. I know of a major law firm in New York that does a lot of work in helping entertainers, performance companies, and restaurants serialize income stream. They work with investment banking firms like ours to sell this type of investment.

For a company, the advantage is that they can sell a film as an investment package with a revenue stream that comes from licensing, foreign sales, videos, and anything else, and cut that up for a professional investment firm to sell as an investment. This gives them income today, through the sale to investors who each get a piece of the interest, and then money as dividends over a certain period of time. At some point, the investment may be rolled over into another investment, or sold out.

As these transactions evolve, there is a need for business research, since the investment bank or security dealer involved must perform due diligence, learning all they can about the individual performer and the liabilities involved. Judgments may have to be made that involve knowing about the chance that an industry is going to survive or die, or that a person's no longer going to be popular. I'm asked many investment-related questions that are really business and public records research questions.

Let's talk about quality and reliability issues. How do you think about the Internet vs. traditional or commercial systems?

Generally, the wider the scope and deeper the coverage, the better will be the research results. Given sufficient time and money, the broader the range of sources that can be used to confirm and verify the data, the better the end result. Very seldom can you comprehensively research a project on the Internet alone, or in print alone, or even through traditional online alone. In today's world, you still need to pick and choose the best sources.

You also need to use all available tools because there is no single source—and usually no single right answer—that you can be certain is authoritative, reliable, and up to date. The paradigm I use involves three factors: money (cost), time (speed), and authority (quality). Generally, I feel that one can have two, but not all three. This means that you can use the Internet for low cost, but possibly trade off quality and speed—not only the slowness of the Web, but because you have so much information to sort through. Alternatively, you can use a high-cost proprietary database with assured quality and fast speed.

By applying this paradigm to every research question, I can recommend what mix of print, traditional online, and Internet resources to use. On the Internet, accuracy and reliability of the data is in question. Information is often lacking about how frequently material is updated. Often, you do not know who or how well-qualified the person you're relying upon is, unless you know what organization the information is coming from or what perspective the author is taking. There are also many biases. Some of the bias is intentional, while some is unintentional and may not be clear. You constantly have to make judgments.

One of the reasons I know that commercial databases are better than much of what is on the Internet is that I go to trade shows and meetings and see product demos. Vendors visit my office regularly. I have no objection to spending the time letting them give me their best pitch and explanation of their product, because they have much to share. I sit on focus groups and don't mind being a beta tester or experimenting with a product, because the vendor is going to get something out of it, and I'm going to be a little further along in my learning curve.

I may never use some of the products, but by being aware of new tools, I will be a better information professional and can share the information with others. I have been chair of the Emerging Technologies Roundtable sponsored by the Legal Division at the annual convention of the Special Libraries Association (SLA) [206], and I have collected and read a great deal about emerging technologies. I will never use many of the tools I was exposed to, but because I'm willing to read and take the time to learn, I'm able to find out about new areas. That helps me do a better job in my day-to-day job as well as in my professional life.

Do you have any success stories about how research saved the day, saved money, or really helped in some way?

In one situation, I was asked to check out whether someone was legitimate. I found out that the person represented an organization that had worked with other major investment banking firms with very good results, and thereafter we became involved with him.

In another example, someone in the middle of a deal said he had a funny feeling that someone might be hiding something. Nobody had done any in-depth research on that person until that time. Lo and behold, in my research, I found a number of outstanding lawsuits and a threat of litigation regarding the underlying property that was the subject of the deal. Naturally, this required some changes to the deal as the attorney rushed to reorganize and set up a whole new series of checks and balances to protect our interests.

They might never have structured these changes if my research hadn't uncovered a background of problems, especially since the person they were dealing with wasn't up-front about the details. The people in the business unit had done their normal research but did not do detailed background research to dig underneath and find out whether problems existed. Through online research, I found quite a number of lawsuits against this person. I also found tax liens and liens filed regarding employees' social security and workers' compensation payments. I found that one of the corporations involved had let its charter lapse.

What are some of the global or macro economic trends that are changing or increasing the need for investment research?

As a general rule, the world is getting faster and more complicated. The number of variables that might affect any one decision is increasing. The need to understand the world, the economy, and all those variables is growing. These changes make research and researchers more important. It's hard to act by the seat of the pants or from one's natural knowledge when making a decision regarding investments. You have to understand and carry out your due diligence obligation in a legal sense. That involves researching and understanding the underlying activity.

Electronic research both helps and hinders our ability to comprehensively understand the world and its activities. It helps by making available to individuals—at their fingertips—greater amounts of information than they ever would have been able to access in a traditional print world. On the other hand, it can produce information overload and the recognition that you ultimately can't understand all the variables or really be certain of anything.

You may throw your hands up and say, "Gee, it's a pretty annual report—let's buy this stock."

You may read huge SEC and EDGAR filings, get 13 different analysts' reports about the same company, do a news search in Lexis-Nexis, Dialog, and Dow Jones, read Bloomberg's Analytics, and look at ADP and D&B Credit Reports. You do all that and you say, "Huh, I can't make hide nor hair of it." Everybody disagrees and you say, "Uh … who knows?" Information delivery to your desktop can be either a wonderfully empowering or a dangerously confounding experience. It can impart knowledge to an individual who may never have had access to it before, or it can drown a person in a sea of information.

Do you think that individual investors will benefit, on the whole, from all the easy-to-use sources for making investment decisions?

Individual investors can get meaningful information that is authoritative and reliable, but a lot of information they come across consists of irresponsible rumors, or disingenuous, inaccurate, or biased information. One big problem area now is stock market fraud based on Internet chat room conversations and phony Web sites that people put up about a company. These are intended to "fake out" investors. People sometimes talk up stocks that they're selling short so they can profit. There is potential for danger to the whole system, which is why the SEC has criticized as irresponsible the advertising by some of the major online trading companies.

Do you have any recommendations or cautionary tales for those just starting out in investment research?

Recognize that a wide variety of sources exists to assist in answering questions, but that they vary widely in accuracy, authority, reliability, and timeliness. Use extreme care with any source before determining its value. Never rely too heavily on any one source. Read as much and as widely as you can. Talk to people. Most especially, ask questions and then listen to the answers. There is a great network of wonderful teachers and mentors out there just waiting to be tapped.

The opinions expressed by me in this interview are my opinions alone and do not in any way reflect or indicate the opinions of Credit Suisse First Boston. All the ideas and statements made during this interview are solely and uniquely mine and should not be interpreted to be those of Credit Suisse First Boston. All products and companies mentioned in the interview reflect my individual and personal opinions and are not in any way the opinions of Credit Suisse First Boston. Nothing I say should be considered an endorsement of any particular product or company.

—Nathan Rosen

Super Searcher Power Tips and Wisdom

➤ The World Bank and some nonprofit institutes and organizations have made an effort to collect information about environmentally sound or public-spirited companies.

➤ Which SEC system we use often depends on its output options. Sometimes you want just a simple list of filings; sometimes you want a summary of the annual report or a more visually attractive or hyperlinked presentation.

➤ Given sufficient time and money, the broader the range of sources that can be used to confirm and verify the data, the better the end result.

➤ You need to use all available tools because there is no one answer, no one source, or one right answer.

Appendix A:
Referenced Sites and Sources

1. **ADP**
   www.adp.com

2. **Alexa**
   www.alexa.com

3. **AltaVista**
   www.altavista.com

4. *American Banker*
   www.americanbanker.com

5. *American Libraries*
   www.ala.org/alonline

6. **American Library Association**
   www.ala.org

7. **America Online (AOL)**
   www.aol.com

8. **Ameritrade**
   www.ameritrade.com

9. **AP (Associated Press)**
   www.ap.org

10. *Asian Venture Capital Journal*
    AVCJ Holdings, Monthly
    www.asiaventure.com

11. **Asset Alternatives, Inc.**
    www.assetalt.com

12. **Association of Certified Fraud Examiners**
    www.cfenet.com

13. **Association for Investment Management and Research (AIMR)**
www.aimr.org

14. **Ballard Spahr**
www.ballardspahr.com

15. **Bank for International Settlements (BIS)**
www.bis.org

16. **Banker's Trust**
www.bankerstrust.com/dbbt

17. **Barra**
www.barra.com

18. **Barron's**
www.barrons.com

19. **Bloomberg**
www.bloomberg.com

20. **Bond Market Association**
www.bondmarket.com

21. **Bridge Station**
www.bridge.com

22. **Bureau of Economic Analysis (BEA)**
www.bea.doc.gov

23. **Business 2.0**
www.business2.com

24. **Business & Industry Database (Dialog File 9)**
www.dialog.com

25. *Business Week*
www.businessweek.com

26. **BUSLIB-L (Business Librarians)**
To subscribe, send email to:
listserv@listserv.boisestate.edu
In body of message type:
Subscribe Buslib-L Your Complete Name

27. *C&RL News* **(College & Research Libraries)**
www.ala.org/acrl/c&rlnew2.html

28. **Canada Stockwatch**
www.canada-stockwatch.com

29. **Capital Institutional Services, Inc.**
www.capis.com

30. **CARL UnCover**
uncweb.carl.org

31. **Cassandra's Revenge**
www.cassandrasrevenge.com

32. **CDA/Spectrum**
www.cda.com

33. **CDB-Infotek (ChoicePoint)**
www.cdb.com

34. **Charles Schwab**
www.schwab.com

35. **CNBC**
www.cnbc.com

36. **CNET News.com**
news.cnet.com/news

37. **CNNFinancial (CNNfn)**
cnnfn.com

38. **COMDEX**
www.zdevents.com/comdex

39. **Commerce Clearing House (CCH)**
business.cch.com

40. **Companies House**
www.companies-house.gov.uk

41. **CompanySleuth**
www.companysleuth.com

42. **Compliance International**
www.complianceintl.com

43. **Compustat (Standard & Poor's)**
www.compustat.com/www

44. **CorporateInformation.com**
www.corporateinformation.com

45. **CorpTech**
www.corptech.com

46. **Court Express (RIS Legal Services)**
www.courtexpress.com

47. **CourtLink**
www.courtlink.com

48. **Data Downlink (.xls)**
www.xls.com

49. **Datamonitor**
www.datamonitor.com

50. **Datastream**
www.datastream.com

51. **Dearborn Financial Publishing**
www.dearborn.com

52. **Dialog**
www.dialog.com

53. **Disclosure Global Access**
www.disclosure.com

54. **Disclosure for Individual Investors**
www.disclosure-investor.com

55. **Donaldson Lufkin & Jenrette**
www.dlj.com

56. **Dow Jones Interactive**
djinteractive.com

57. **DRI (Standard & Poor's)**
www.dri.mcgraw-hill.com

58. **Dun & Bradstreet**
www.dnb.com

59. **ECINVESTOR**
www.ecinvestor.com

60. *The Economist*
www.economist.com

61. **Economist Intelligence Unit's (EIU) Country Reports**
www.eiu.com

62. *EContent*
Online, Inc., bimonthly
www.ecmag.net

63. **Education Index**
HW Wilson Company
www.hwwilson.com

64. **Edupage**
www.ee.surrey.ac.uk/Contrib/Edupage

65. **ERIC (Dialog File 1)**
www.dialog.com

66. **E*TRADE**
www.etrade.com

67. *Euromoney*
Euromoney Publications, Monthly
www.euromoney.com

68. **European Business Information Conference (EBIC)**
www.tfpl.com/bic/conferences_fr1.htm

69. **Excite**
www.excite.com

70. **Extel**
www.primark.com/pfid/content/extel.shtml

71. **FactSet**
www.factset.com

72. **FDIC (Federal Deposit Insurance Corporation)**
www.fdic.gov

73. **Federal Filings, Inc.**
www.fedfil.com/ipo/index.html

74. **Federal Reserve**
www.federalreserve.gov

75. **Fedlink**
lcweb.loc.gov/flicc/

76. **Financial Research Corporation**
www.fdinet.com/SCONSUL3.HTM

77. *Financial Times*
www.ft.com

78. **Find/SVP**
www.findsvp.com

79. **First Call**
www.1firstcall.com

80. **FISonline**
www.fisonline.com

81. **Flow of Cash Funds**
www.bog.frb.fed.us/releases/Z1

82. **Forrester Research**
www.forrester.com

83. *Fortune*
www.fortune.com

84. **FreeEDGAR**
www.freeedgar.com

85. **Galante's Venture Capital & Private Equity Directory**
www.assetalt.com/products/dir/index.htm

86. **Gale Group F&S Index (Dialog File 18)**
www.dialog.com

87. **Gale Group Trade & Industry Database (Dialog File 148)**
www.dialog .com

88. **Global Research (St. Louis)**
www.stlglobalre.com

89. **Global Securities Information, Inc.**
www.gsionline.com

90. *Globe and Mail*
www.globeandmail.ca

91. **Goldman Sachs**
www.gs.com

92. **Google**
www.google.com

93. **Harvard University Business School Working Papers**
library.hbs.edu/workpaplink.htm

94. **Haver Analytics**
www.haver.com

95. **Hoover's**
www.hoovers.com

96. **HotBot**
www.hotbot.com

97. **Ibbotson EnCorr**
www.ibbotson.com/Products/software/analysis/default.asp

98. **I/B/E/S**
www.ibes.com

99. **ICI (Investment Company Institute)**
www.ici.org

100. **IDC (Interactive Data Corp.)**
www.intdata.com

101. *Industry Standard*
The Industry Standard, Weekly
www.thestandard.net

102. **Infobeat**
www.infobeat.com

103. **Infomart**
www.infomart.com

104. **Information America**
www.infoam.com

105. *Information Outlook*
Special Libraries Association, Monthly
www.sla.org

106. *Information Today*
Information Today, Inc., Monthly
www.infotoday.com/it/itnew.htm

107. *Informed Librarian*
Infosources Publishing, Monthly
www.infosourcespub.com

108. **Infoseek**
www.infoseek.com

109. *Inside Market Data*
www.watersinfo.com

110. **InSync**
DiBiasio & Edgington
7857 Heritage Drive, Suite 320
Annandale, Virginia 22003
703-642-9200

111. **Intelliscope**
www.intelliscope.com

112. **International Data Corporation (IDC)**
www.idc.com

113. **International Directory of Venture Capital Funds**
Fitzroy Dearborn Publishers
www.fitzroydearborn.com/dirvcf.htm

114. **International Monetary Fund**
www.imf.org/external

115. *Internet Lawyer*
Monthly
www.internetlawyer.com

116. *Internet Newsletter: Legal and Business Aspects*
Leader Publications, Monthly
www.ljx.com/newsletters

117. *InternetWeek*
CMP Media, Inc., Weekly
www.internetwk.com

118. **Internet Wire**
www.internetwire.com

119. *Internet World*
Penton Media, Inc., 42x/year
www.iw.com

120. **Internet World (Conference)**
Penton Media, Inc.
www.penton.com/markets/it/index.html

121. **Investext**
www.investext.com

122. **InvestWorks**
www.barra.com/InvData/PStyleAnalysis.asp

123. **ISI (Institute for Scientific Information)**
Citation Indexes
www.isinet.com

124. **iVillage MoneyLife**
www.ivillagemoneylife.com

125. *Journal of Academic Librarianship*
www.suffolk.edu/admin/sawlib/jal/contents.html

126. **KnowX**
www.knowx.com

127. **Lexis-Nexis**
www.lexis-nexis.com

128. **Lexis-Nexis Academic Universe**
www.cispubs.com/market/universe/univ1.htm

129. *Library Journal*
www.ljdigital.com

130. **Library Literature**
HW Wilson Company
www.hwwilson.com

131. *Library Quarterly*
www.journals.uchicago.edu/LQ/home.html

132. *Library Trends*
www.lis.uiuc.edu/puboff/catalog/trends

133. **Lipper Analytical Services**
www.lipperweb.com

134. **LIVEDGAR**
www.gsionline.com

135. **Lycos**
www.lycos.com

136. **Market Data Professionals, Inc.**
www.market-data.com

137. **Market Guide**
www.marketguide.com/MGI

138. **Market Insight (Standard & Poor's)**
www.compustat.com/www/products/mktinst3.htm

139. **MarketSpan (CaseStream)**
www.casestream.com

140. **Martindale-Hubbell**
www.martindale.com

141. **McDermott, Will & Emery**
www.mwe.com

142. **Media Central**
www.mediacentral.com

143. **Media General**
www.mediageneral.com

144. **Mergerstat**
www.mergerstat.com

145. **Merrill Lynch**
www.merrilllynch.com or www.ml.com

146. **Moody's**
www.moodys.com

147. **Morgan Lewis**
www.mlb.com

148. **Morgan Stanley Dean Witter**
www.ms.com

149. **Morningstar**
www.morningstar.com

150. **Motley Fool**
www.fool.com

151. **MSNBC**
www.msnbc.com/news

152. **Muller Data**
www.muller.com

153. **Multex**
www.multex.com

154. **Mutual Fund Café**
www.mfcafe.com/index.html

155. **NASD (National Association of Securities Dealers)**
www.nasd.com

156. **National Online Meeting**
Information Today, Inc.
www.infotoday.com

157. **National Securities Clearing Corp. (NSCC)**
www.nscc.com

158. **Nelson's Directory of Investment Managers**
www.nelnet.com/catalog/dim.htm

159. **New York Institute of Finance**
www.nyif.com/bookcatalog

160. *New York Law Journal*
www.nylj.com

161. **New York State Banking Department**
www.banking.state.ny.us

162. **New York Stock Exchange**
www.nyse.com

163. *The New York Times*
www.nytimes.com

164. **Newscan**
www.newscan.com

165. **NewsEdge**
www.newsedge.com

166. **Nikkei**
www.nni.nikkei.co.jp

167. **Northern Light**
www.northernlight.com or www.nlsearch.com

168. **Northfield**
www.northinfo.com

169. **OCLC FirstSearch**
www.oclc.org/oclc/menu/eco.htm

170. **OECD (Organisation for Economic Co-operation and Development)**
www.oecd.org

171. **OneSource**
www.onesource.com

172. *ONLINE*
Online, Inc., Bimonthly
www.onlineinc.com

173. **PACER (Public Access to Court Electronics Records)**
pacer.psc.uscourts.gov

174. **Philadelphia Stock Exchange**
www.phlx.com/index.stm

175. ***Pratt's Guide to Venture Capital Sources 1999* (23rd Edition)**
Stanley E. Pratt, Editor
Venture Economics, ISBN: 0914470973

176. **Primark Global Information Services**
www.primark.com

177. *The Private Equity Analyst's Newsletter*
Asset Alternatives, Inc., Monthly
assetalt.com/products/news/pea.htm

178. **PROMT (Dialog File 16)**
www.dialog.com

179. **ProQuest**
www.umi.com/proquest or www.proquest.com

180. **PSN (Plan Sponsor Network)**
www.informa.com/Informa/Pages/Display.ASP?file_name=product_
info_32.XML

181. **Quicklaw**
www.qlsys.ca

182. **Quote.com**
www.quote.com/index.html

183. **Raging Bull**
www.ragingbull.com

184. *Red Herring*
Red Herring Communications, San Francisco, CA, Monthly
www.herring.com

185. *Reference and User Services Quarterly*
www.ala.org/rusa/rusq

186. *Reference Services Review (RSR)*
olive.harvard.edu:81/ejournals

187. **Research Bank Web (Investext)**
www.investext.com

188. **Reuters**
www.reuters.com

189. **Russell Performance Universe**
russell.com

190. **Salomon Yield Book**
www.smithbarney.com/capmark/instit/gpb_rsrchsvc.htm

191. **SAS**
www.sas.com

192. *Scout Report*
scout.cs.wisc.edu/report/sr/current/index.html

193. **Search Engine Watch and** *Search Engine Report*
Danny Sullivan, Editor, Monthly
searchenginewatch.com

194. *Searcher Magazine*
Information Today, Inc., 10x/year
www.infotoday.com/searcher

195. *Seattle Times*
www.seattletimes.com

196. **SEC (Securities and Exchange Commission)**
www.sec.gov

197. *Secrets of the Super Net Searchers*
Reva Basch, CyberAge Books, Information Today, Inc., 1996
www.infotoday.com/catalog/books.htm

198. **Securities Class Action Clearing Center**
securities.stanford.edu/index.html

199. **Securities Data Corp. (SDC), now Thomson Financial Securities Data**
www.tfsd.com

200. **Securities Industry Association**
www.sia.com

201. **SEDAR**
www.sedar.com

202. **SiebertNet**
www.siebertnet.com

203. **Silicon Investor**
www.siliconinvestor.com

204. *SmartMoney*
www.smartmoney.com

205. **SNL Securities**
www.snlsecurities.com

206. **Special Libraries Association (SLA)**
www.sla.org

207. **Standard & Poor's**
www.standardpoor.com or www.standardandpoors.com

208. **Statistical Abstract of the United States**
http://www.census.gov/prod/3/98pubs/98statab/cc98stab.htm

209. **Stock Point**
www.stockpoint.com

210. **Stocksite, now Silicon Investor**
www.siliconinvestor.com

211. **Sybase**
www.sybase.com

212. **Teikoku**
www.teikoku.com

213. **Telerate Plus**
www.telerate.com

214. **TheStreet.com**
www.thestreet.com

215. **Thomson Financial**
www.tfp.com

216. *Trading Technology Week*
www.watersinfo.com

217. **United Nations**
www.un.org

218. **United States Bureau of the Census**
www.census.gov

219. **University of Cincinnati College of Law Center for Corporate Law**
taft.law.uc.edu/CCL

220. **UPI (United Press International)**
www.upi.com

221. *Upside*
Upside Media, Inc., Monthly
www.upside.com

222. **U.S. Bancorp Piper Jaffray**
www.piperjaffray.com

223. **Value Line**
www.valueline.com

224. **Venture One**
www.ventureone.com

225. **Vision** (Innovative Systems Techniques - Insyte)
www.insytenet.com

226. *The Wall Street Journal*
www.wsj.com

227. ***The Wall Street Journal Guide to Understanding***
     Money and Investments
     Kenneth M. Morris, Virginia B. Morris, Alan M. Siegel, August 1999
     Fireside; ISBN: 0684869020

228. **Wall Street Research Network (WSRN)**
     www.wsrn.com

229. **Waterhouse Securities, Inc.**
     www.waterhouse.com

230. **Waters Information Services**
     www.watersinfo.com

231. **WebCrawler**
     www.webcrawler.com

232. **Westlaw**
     www.westlaw.com

233. **Wharton School, University of Pennsylvania**
     www.wharton.upenn.edu

234. **White House Economic Statistics Briefing Room**
     www.whitehouse.gov/fsbr/esbr.html

235. **Wilshire**
     www.wilshire.com

236. **Women's Institute for Financial Education (WIFE)**
     www.wife.com

237. **Women's Wire**
     www.womenswire.com

238. **World Bank**
     www.worldbank.org

239. **Worldscope**
     www.primark.com/pfid/content/worldscope.shtml

240. **Yahoo!**
     www.yahoo.com

241. **Yahoo! Finance**
     finance.yahoo.com or quote.yahoo.com

242. **Zacks Investment Research**
     www.zacks.com

Appendix B:
Glossary of Terms

Acoustic Coupler. A device onto which a telephone handset is placed to connect a computer with a network. The acoustic coupler might also contain a modem, or the modem could be a separate device. Popular in the 1970s, acoustic couplers are no longer widely used.

AOL. America Online. A consumer-oriented online service.

Archie. An Internet search tool, primarily for FTP sites and archives.

Ask Price. The lowest price that any investor or dealer has declared that he or she will sell a given security or commodity for. For over-the-counter stocks, the ask is the best quoted price at which a market maker is willing to sell a stock. For mutual funds, the ask is the net asset value plus any sales charges. Also called *asked price* or *asking price* or *offering price*.

Asset Allocation. The process of dividing investments among different kinds of assets, such as stocks, bonds, real estate and cash, to optimize the risk/reward trade-off based on an individual's or institution's specific situation and goals.

Benchmark. A standard used for comparison.

Bid Price. The highest price any buyer is willing to pay for a given security at a given time.

Blue Chip. Stock of a large, national company with a solid record of stable earnings and/or dividend growth, and a reputation for high-quality management and/or products.

Boolean Logic. Named after 19th-century mathematician George Boole, Boolean logic is a form of algebra in which all values are reduced to either TRUE or FALSE. The Boolean operators AND, OR, and NOT are used for searching professional online database services such as Dialog, Dow Jones, and Lexis-Nexis.

Brokerage. A brokerage firm executes trades for its clients and provides research and advice. Used interchangeably with *broker* when referring to a firm rather than an individual. Also called *brokerage house* or *brokerage firm*.

Buy Side. The investment management/money management business, which comprises all the institutional buyers. Can be a department within a full service investment bank (such as an investment management department) or a separate firm dedicated to that business.

Buyout. The purchase of controlling interest in one corporation by another corporation, in order to take over assets and/or operations.

Capital. Cash or goods used to generate income. Also, the net worth of a business, i.e., the amount by which its assets exceed its liabilities.

Capitalization. The sum of a corporation's long-term debt, stock and retained earnings. Also called *invested capital*. Also, the market price of an entire company, calculated by multiplying the number of shares outstanding by the price per share. Also called *market cap* or *market capitalization*. Corporations are described as large cap, small cap, and so on, on the basis of their market capitalizations:

> Large cap: Over $5 billion
> Mid cap: $500 million to $5 billion
> Small cap: $150 million to $500 million
> Micro cap: Below $150 million

Capitalization Ratio. Also called *financial leverage ratio*, these ratios compare debt to total capitalization and thus reflect the extent to which a corporation is trading on its equity. Capitalization ratios can be interpreted only in the context of the stability of industry and company earnings and cash flow.

Cash. Currency and coins on hand, bank balances, and negotiable money orders and checks.

CD. Certificate of Deposit. Short- or medium-term, interest-bearing, FDIC-insured debt instrument offered by banks and savings and loans.

Classified Stock. The separation of a company's common stock into multiple classes, such as Class A and Class B. Also called *complex capital structure* or *multiple capital structure*.

Closing. The finalizing of the sale of a property, as its title is transferred from the seller to the buyer.

Common Stock. Securities that represent an ownership interest in a corporation. If the company has also issued preferred stock, both common and preferred have ownership rights. Common stockholders assume the greater risk, but generally exercise the greater control and may gain the greater award in the form of dividends and capital appreciation. The terms *common stock* and *capital stock* are often used interchangeably when the company has no preferred stock.

Composite. An index or average that is a combination of multiple other indexes or averages. An example is the Dow Jones Composite, which combines the industrial, transportation, and utility averages.

Comptroller. A company's chief accountant.

Controller. See *comptroller*.

Corporate Finance. One of the three areas of the discipline of finance. It deals with the operation of the firm (both the investment decision and the financing decision) from that firm's point of view.

Credit Derivative. A derivative instrument that transfers credit risk from one party to another.

Debt. A liability or obligation in the form of bonds, loan notes, or mortgages that is owed to another person or persons and is required to be paid by a specified date (maturity).

Debt-to-Equity Ratio. A measure of a company's leverage calculated by dividing long-term debt by common shareholders' equity, usually using the data from the previous fiscal year.

Derivative. A financial instrument whose characteristics and value depend upon the characteristics and value of an underlying instrument or asset, typically a commodity, bond, equity or currency. Examples are futures, options, and mortgage-backed securities.

Dialog Bluesheets. Written guides for individual databases on the Dialog service. Bluesheets include file description, subject coverage, date range, update frequency, sources, and producer information, as well as instructions on searching using the special features of each database.

Disclosure Compact D [www.primark.com/pfid/applications/compactd. shtml]. Four databases proprietary to Primark on CD-ROM or online: Disclosure SEC and Company, Worldscope, Canada, and New Issues.

Dividend. Taxable payment declared by a company's board of directors and given to its shareholders out of the company's current or retained earnings. Dividends are usually paid quarterly and in cash, but can also take the form of stock or other property.

Dividend Reinvestment Plan (DRIP). Investment plan offered by some corporations enabling shareholders to automatically reinvest cash dividends and capital gains distributions, thereby accumulating more stock without paying brokerage commissions. Many DRIPs also allow the investment of additional cash from the shareholder, known as an *optional cash purchase*.

Docket. The cases on a court calendar.

Downgrade. A negative change in ratings for a stock or other rated security.

Due Diligence. The process of investigation performed by or on behalf of investors into the details of a potential investment. Includes an examination of operations and management and the verification of material facts.

EBITDA. Earnings before interest, taxes, depreciation, and amortization.

EDGAR. Electronic Data Gathering, Analysis, and Retrieval. The database of legal filings from the United States Securities and Exchange Commission (SEC), EDGAR performs automated collection, validation, indexing, acceptance, and forwarding of submissions by companies and others required by law to file forms with the SEC. Currently, all domestic (meaning U.S.-domiciled or incorporated) companies are required to file electronically. Foreign private issuers (that is, companies not incorporated in the United States that are not governmental entities) can still file on paper or voluntarily file electronically.

Endowment. A permanent fund bestowed upon an individual or institution, such as a university, museum, hospital, or foundation, to be used for a specific purpose.

Equity. The ownership interest of common and preferred stockholders in a company. Also refers to excess of value of securities over the debit balance in a margin account.

Equity Research. Company and industry research from brokerage firms.

ERISA. Employee Retirement Income Security Act of 1974. The federal law that established legal guidelines for private pension plan administration and investment practices.

FDIC. Federal Deposit Insurance Corporation [www.fdic.gov]. Its mission is to maintain stability of and public confidence in the nation's financial system. To achieve this goal, the FDIC has insured deposits and promoted safe and sound banking practices since 1933.

Fixed Income. A security that pays a specific interest rate, such as a bond, money market instrument, or preferred stock.

FTP. File Transfer Protocol. An Internet-based system for accessing and transferring files to and from remote computers.

Fundamental Analysis. A method of security valuation that involves examining the company's financials and operations, especially sales, earnings, growth potential, assets, debt, management, products, and competition.

Futures. A standardized, transferable, exchange-traded contract that requires delivery of a commodity, bond, currency, or stock index at a specified price on a specified future date.

GAAP. Generally Accepted Accounting Principles. A widely accepted set of rules, conventions, standards, and procedures for reporting financial information as established by the Financial Accounting Standards Board.

GDP. Gross Domestic Product. The total market value of all final goods and services produced in a country in a given year; equals total consumer, investment, and government spending, plus the value of exports minus the value of imports.

Gopher. A menu-based system for providing access to collections of data across the Internet. Less prevalent since the advent of the World Wide Web.

Gopherspace. The sum of all gophers and the information contained therein.

Growth Style. The word *growth*, in the context of investing, can be used to describe companies, stocks, or mutual funds, all of which are related to each other. Typically, a growth-style mutual fund will own growth stocks representing companies currently in an earnings growth phase. If corporate earnings begin to slow down or reverse, however, that company and its stock may no longer be considered to represent a growth opportunity.

High. The highest price paid for a security during a certain time period.

Holding Company. A company that owns enough voting stock in another firm to control management and operations by influencing or electing its board of directors. Also called *parent company*.

HTML. HyperText Markup Language, the authoring language used to create documents on the World Wide Web.

Indenture. A written agreement between the issuer of a bond and the bondholders, usually specifying interest rate, maturity date, convertibility, and other terms.

Institutional Investor. Entity with large amounts to invest, such as investment companies, mutual funds, brokerages, insurance companies, pension funds, investment banks, and endowment funds. Institutional investors are covered by fewer protective regulations because it is assumed that they are more knowledgeable and better able to protect themselves. Institutional investors account for a majority of overall trading volume.

Instrument. A document containing some legal right or obligation. Examples include notes, agreements, and contracts.

Investment Trust. A closed-end fund established to produce income through investments. Investment trusts have a fixed number of shares and trade-like stocks, and they are regulated by the Investment Company Act of 1940.

Initial Public Offering (IPO). The first sale of stock by a company to the public.

IRA. Individual Retirement Account. A tax-deferred retirement account that permits individuals to set aside up to $2,000 per year, with earnings tax-deferred until withdrawals begin at age 59 1/2 or later (or earlier, with a 10% penalty).

ISDN. Integrated Services Digital Network, an international communications standard for sending voice, video, and data over telephone lines.

Issue. Stock or bond offered for sale by a corporation or government entity, usually through an underwriter or in a private placement.

Knowledge Management. The process of capturing a company's collective expertise wherever it resides—in databases, on paper, or in the minds of employees—and disseminating it to areas within the company where it can help produce the biggest payoff.

LAN. Local Area Network. A computer network that spans a relatively small area.

Large Cap. See *capitalization*.

Lexis-Nexis ALLBIZ. The ALLBIZ group file combines the following files:

Corporation and limited partnership filings
"Doing Business As" (DBA)
California Contractor State License Board Information
California State Board of Equalization Sales and Use Tax Permit Holder
  Information
Texas Comptroller's Office Sales and Use Tax Permit Holder Information
Franchise Index.

Lexis-Nexis ALLNWS. The Lexis-Nexis News library contains news sources available in the Nexis service. The ALLNWS group file contains complete archival files.

Lexis-Nexis ALLOWN. ALLOWN is a group file of tax assessor, deed transfer and mortgage records for selected states and counties. Although individual records may vary in content, most documents include the following:

Owner, buyer and/or seller name(s)
Property and/or mailing address
Assessor parcel number
Property use

Lexis-Nexis ONPROP. A database of the Ontario, Canada, property file with tax assessor property information records for all Ontario, Canada, counties/regions/districts.

Loan Participation. A loan shared by a group of banks that join to lend an amount greater than any of the participants could commit to individually.

Low. The lowest price reached by a security or commodity in a certain period of time, usually a single trading session (here, also called *daily low*).

Manager. The person(s) responsible for overall strategy and specific buying and selling decisions for a mutual fund (called a *fund manager*) or other financial institution (called a *money manager*).

Market Cap. See *capitalization*.

Market Maker. Brokerage or bank that maintains a firm bid and ask price in a given over-the-counter security by standing ready, willing, and able to buy or sell at publicly quoted prices (called *making a market*).

Material Event. Information that would be likely to affect a stock's price once it becomes known to the public. Examples include a takeover, a divestiture, significant management changes, and new product introductions.

Metasearch Engines. Internet search engines that submit a search query to several individual search engines at one time.

Metasites. Web sites that function as a directory or set of pointers to other Web sites.

Mezzanine Financing. Late-stage venture capital, usually the final round of financing prior to an IPO.

Mid Cap. See *capitalization*.

M.L.S. or M.L.I.S. Master of Library Science or Master of Library and Information Science degree.

Money Management. The process of managing money, including investments, budgeting, banking, and taxes. Also called *portfolio management* or *investment management.*

Multiple. Method of evaluating a stock's desirability by dividing the stock price by the earnings per share.

Mutual Fund. Pools of money that are managed by an investment company that raises money from shareholders and invests in a group of assets in accordance with a stated set of objectives. Benefits include diversification and professional money management.

NASD. National Association of Securities Dealers. A self-regulatory securities industry organization responsible for the operation and regulation of the NASDAQ stock market and over-the-counter markets.

NASDAQ. National Association of Securities Dealers Automated Quotations system. A computerized system established by the NASD to facilitate trading by providing broker/dealers with current bid and ask price quotes on over-the-counter stocks and some listed stocks.

Net Asset Value (NAV). The dollar value of a single mutual fund share, based on the value of the underlying assets of the fund minus its liabilities, divided by the number of shares outstanding. Calculated at the end of each business day.

Newsgroup. An Internet-based topical discussion group, generally part of the Usenet hierarchy.

Open-End Fund. Same as mutual fund. A closed-end fund is often incorrectly referred to as a mutual fund, but is actually an investment trust.

Optimization. Putting together a portfolio in such a way as to maximize return for a given risk level or to minimize risk for a given expected-return level.

Option. The right, but not the obligation, to buy (for a *call option*) or sell (for a *put option*) a specific amount of a given stock, commodity, currency, index, or debt, at a specified price (the *strike price*) during a specified period of time. For stock options, the amount is usually 100 shares.

Over-the-Counter (OTC). A security that is not traded on an exchange, usually due to an inability to meet listing requirements. For such securities, broker/dealers negotiate directly with one another over computer networks and by phone, and their activities are monitored by the NASD.

PDF. Portable Document Format. A proprietary digital file format developed by Adobe Systems. PDF makes it possible to exchange documents and view them as originally intended, with all formatting intact. Viewing PDF files requires Acrobat Reader, a free application distributed by Adobe Systems.

Penny Stock. Extremely speculative, high-risk stock, usually with a price of less than one dollar per share. Frequently used as a term of disparagement, although some penny stocks have developed into investment-caliber issues.

Pension Plan. A qualified retirement plan set up by a corporation, labor union, government, or other organization for its employees. Examples include profit-sharing plans, stock bonus and Employee Stock Ownership Plans (ESOPs), thrift plans, target benefit plans, money purchase plans, and defined benefit plans.

Performance. The results of activities of an organization or investment over a given period of time.

Plan Sponsor. An employer who sets up a pension plan.

Portfolio. A collection of investments owned by an individual or organization.

Preferred Stock. A class of stock with a claim on the company's earnings before payment is made on the common stock, and usually entitled to priority over common stock if the company liquidates. Usually entitled to dividends at a specified rate—when declared by the Board of Directors and before payment of a dividend on the common stock—depending upon the terms of the issue.

P/E Ratio. Price-to-Earnings Ratio. The most common measure of how expensive a stock is. The P/E ratio is the price of a share of stock divided by earnings per share for a 12-month period.

Private Placement. The sale of securities directly to institutional investors, such as banks, mutual funds, insurance companies, pension funds, and foundations. Does not require SEC registration provided the securities are bought for investment purposes rather than resale, as specified in the investment letter.

Profit-Sharing. An arrangement in which an employer shares its profits with its employees. The compensation can be stocks, bonds, or cash, and can be immediate or deferred until retirement.

Prospectus. A legal document offering securities or mutual fund shares for sale required by the Securities Act of 1933. The prospectus must explain the offer, including the terms, issuer, objectives (if mutual fund) or planned use of the money (if securities); historical financial statements;

and other information that could help individuals decide whether the investment is appropriate for them.

Proxy. A written authorization given by a shareholder for someone else, usually the company's management, to cast his or her vote at a shareholder meeting or at another time.

Proxy Contest/Proxy Fight. Takeover technique in which the acquirer tries to persuade the target company's shareholders to vote for a board of directors who accept the takeover.

Ratio. One value divided by another. Examples: price/earnings ratio, quick ratio, loan/value ratio, advertising sales ratio, asset/equity ratio, bid-to-cover ratio, book-to-bill ratio, cash ratio, cash asset ratio, common stock ratio, conversion ratio, coverage ratio, current ratio, debt ratio, debt/equity ratio, exercise ratio, expense ratio, fixed-charge coverage ratio, and more.

REIT. Real Estate Investment Trust. A corporation or trust that uses the pooled capital of many investors to purchase and manage income property (*equity REIT*) and/or mortgage loans (*mortgage REIT*). REITs are often publicly held.

Reorganization. The implementation of a business plan to restructure a corporation, which may include transfers of stock between shareholders of two corporations in a merger. In bankruptcy, a corporation in deep financial trouble may be given time to reorganize while protected from creditors by the bankruptcy court.

Risk Management. The process of analyzing exposure to risk and determining how to best handle such exposure. *Risk* is defined as the quantifiable likelihood of loss or less-than-expected returns.

SEC. Securities and Exchange Commission. The primary U.S. federal regulatory agency for the securities industry, with responsibility to promote full disclosure and to protect investors against fraudulent and manipulative practices in the securities markets. The SEC enforces, among other acts, the Securities Act of 1933, the Securities Exchange Act of 1934, the Trust Indenture Act of 1939, the Investment Company Act of 1940, and the Investment Advisers Act. The supervision of dealers is delegated to the self-regulatory bodies of the exchanges.

SEC Form 3. A document required by the SEC and the appropriate stock exchange to announce the holdings of directors, officers, and shareholders owning 10% or more of the company's outstanding stock.

SEC Form 8-K. A document required by the SEC to announce certain significant changes in a public company, such as a merger or acquisition, a name or address change, bankruptcy, change of auditors, or any other information that a potential investor ought to know about. It provides more current information on certain specified events than would Forms 10-Q or 10-K. It must be filed within 15 days of any event specified in the form (except for Item 5).

SEC Form 10-K. Same as annual report, which most reporting companies file with the SEC. It provides a comprehensive overview of the registrant's business. The report must be filed within 90 days after the end of the company's fiscal year.

SEC Form 10-Q. Same as quarterly report, which most reporting companies file. It includes unaudited financial statements and provides a continuing view of the company's financial position during the year. The report must be filed for each of the first three fiscal quarters and is due within 45 days of the close of the quarter.

SEC Form S-1. A registration statement used in the initial public offering of securities.

SEC Rule 13d. An SEC rule requiring disclosure by anyone acquiring a beneficial ownership of 5% or more of any equity security registered with the SEC. If the company is listed on an exchange, the form must be filed with the exchange, too. A Schedule 13d form must be filed according to Rule 13d.

Securities Act of 1933. First Congressional law regulating the securities industry. The law required registration and disclosure and included measures to discourage fraud and deception.

Securities Exchange Act of 1934. The act that created the SEC; outlawed manipulative and abusive practices in the issuance of securities; required registration of stock exchanges, brokers, dealers, and listed securities, and required disclosure of certain financial information and insider trading.

Securities Industry Association (SIA). The principal trade association and lobbying group for broker/dealers.

Security. An investment instrument, other than an insurance policy or fixed annuity, issued by a corporation, government, or other organization, which offers evidence of debt or equity.

Selling Short. See *short selling*.

Share. Certificate representing one unit of ownership in a corporation, mutual fund, or limited partnership.

Shareholder. One who owns shares of stock in a corporation or mutual fund. For corporations, along with the ownership comes a right to declare dividends and to vote on certain company matters, including the board of directors. Also called *stockholder*.

Shell. A corporation with no real assets or operations; sometimes fraudulent.

Short Selling. Establishing a market position by selling a security one does not own in anticipation of the price of that security falling

SIC. Standard Industrial Classification code. Four-digit codes established by the U.S. government and used to categorize and uniquely identify business activities. The SIC system is in the process of being replaced by the North American Industry Classification System (NAICS), which was developed jointly by the U.S., Canada, and Mexico to provide new comparability in statistics about business activity across North America.

Skip Tracing. Finding individuals who have skipped out without paying their bills and other obligations.

SLA. Special Libraries Association [www.sla.org]. An international professional association that represents nearly 15,000 information resource experts who collect, analyze, evaluate, package, and disseminate information to facilitate accurate decision-making. SLA's members are employed by corporations, private companies, government agencies, technical and academic institutions, museums, medical facilities, and information management consulting firms.

Small Cap. See *capitalization*.

Spinoff. An independent company created from an existing part of another company through a divestiture, such as a sale or distribution of new shares.

SRO. Self-regulatory organization. Non-government organization that has statutory responsibility to regulate its own members through the adoption and enforcement of rules of conduct for fair, ethical, and efficient practices. Examples include NASD and the National Securities and Commodities Exchanges.

Stock. An instrument that signifies an ownership position, or equity, in a corporation and represents a claim on its proportionate share in the corporation's assets and profits.

Stock Symbol. A unique letter symbol assigned to a security. For U.S. securities, one-, two-, and three-letter symbols indicate that the security is listed and trades on an exchange.

Stop Words. Common words such as "the," "corp.," and "inc." which a search engine ignores when processing a search request. Stop words cannot be used as search terms.

Time Series. A sequence of observations that are ordered in time (or space). For example, weekly share prices or monthly profits.

T-1. A dedicated high-speed telephone connection supporting data transfer rates of 1.544 Mbits per second. T-1 lines are a popular leased line option for businesses connecting to the Internet and for Internet Service Providers (ISPs) connecting to the Internet backbone. The Internet backbone itself consists of faster T-3 connections.

Telnet. Internet standard protocol for connecting to and interacting with a remote computer.

Tender. To offer for delivery, as of a futures contract. Also, to surrender one's shares in return for payment following a *tender offer*.

Tender Offer. A takeover bid in the form of a public invitation to shareholders to sell their stock, generally at a price above the market price.

Ticker Symbol. A system of letters used to uniquely identify a stock or mutual fund. Symbols with up to three letters are used for stocks that are listed and traded on an exchange. Symbols with four letters are used for NASDAQ stocks. Symbols with five letters are used for NASDAQ stocks other than single issues of common stock. Symbols with five letters ending in X are used for mutual funds.

Tier. A class or group of securities.

UCC. Uniform Commercial Code. A business code that has been adopted as law in most states. The UCC governs commercial transactions (sale of goods, ownership) concerning personal property. Also, a financing agreement form for using personal property (e.g. equipment) to secure a loan under the provisions of the Uniform Commercial Code (UCC) adopted in almost all states.

URL. Uniform Resource Locator. The address of a Web page or other Internet resource.

Underwriter. An intermediary between an issuer of a security and the investing public, usually an investment bank.

Underwriting. The procedure by which an underwriter brings a new security issue to the investing public in an offering. Also, the process of insuring someone or something.

Upgrade. A positive change in ratings for a security. Two common examples are an analyst's upgrading a stock (such as from "sell" to "buy") and a credit bureau's upgrading of a bond.

Usenet. A collection of thousands of online discussion groups, plus the computers that host them and the user population that participates in them. Also known as *newsgroups*.

Valuation. The process of determining the value of an asset or company.

Value at Risk. The methodology that measures the sensitivity of a portfolio or firm's position with parametric statistical techniques. It uses historical information to estimate the impact of various standard deviation events upon the value of the holdings and the associated impact on earnings.

Value Investing. An investment style that favors good stocks at great prices over great stocks at good prices. Utilizes such valuation measures as price to book ratio, price/earnings ratio, and yield.

Veronica. A comprehensive *gopher* search tool covering all or most of gopherspace at the menu or filename level.

WAN. Wide Area Network. A computer network that spans a relatively large geographical area. Typically, a WAN consists of two or more local area networks (LANs). Computers connected to a wide area network are often connected through public networks, such as the telephone system. They can also be connected through leased lines or satellites. The largest WAN in existence is the Internet.

Web Portal. A Web site or service that offers a broad array of resources and services, such as e-mail, forums, search engines, and online shopping malls.

GLOSSARY SOURCES

Investorwords
www.investorwords.com

Money Words
www.moneywords.com

Onelook Dictionaries
www.onelook.com

Series 7 General Securities Representative License Exam Manual (10th Edition, 1998).
Dearborn Financial Publishing, Chicago, IL.
www.dearborn.com

TechEncyclopedia
www.techweb.com/encyclopedia

Webopedia (internet.com)
www.webopedia.internet.com

WellsTrade
Wells Fargo Securities Online Brokerage
www.wellsfargo.com/wellstrade/glossary/

Yahoo! Financial Glossary
www.biz.yahoo.com/f/g/g.html

About the Author

Amelia Kassel is President and owner of MarketingBASE, a successful information brokerage specializing since 1984 in market research, competitive intelligence, and worldwide business information. Kassel, who earned a Master's degree in Library Science from UCLA in 1971, combines an in-depth knowledge of information sources and electronic databases with business and marketing strategies. She has taught for more than 15 years at the graduate level and currently teaches a course on "How to Conduct Internet Research for Competitive and Market Intelligence" at the University of California, Berkeley Extension Marketing Program.

A recognized author and national and international speaker, Kassel conducts online research seminars and workshops for numerous conferences and associations. She also operates the Information Broker Mentor Program (www.marketingbase.com)—a distance education program used by independent and corporate researchers worldwide.

About the Editor

Reva Basch, executive editor of the Super Searchers series, is a writer, researcher, and consultant to the online industry. She is the author of the original Super Searcher books, *Secrets of the Super Searchers* and *Secrets of the Super Net Searchers*, as well as *Researching Online For Dummies* and *Electronic Information Delivery: Ensuring Quality and Value*. She writes the "Reva's (W)rap" column for *ONLINE* magazine, has contributed numerous articles and columns to professional journals and the popular press, and has keynoted at conferences in Europe, Scandinavia, Australia, Canada, and the U.S.

A past president of the Association of Independent Information Professionals, she has a Master's in Library Science from the University of California at Berkeley and more than 20 years of experience in database and Internet research. Basch was Vice President and Director of Research at Information on Demand and has been president of her own company, Aubergine Information Services, since 1986.

Index

More CyberAge Books
from Information Today, Inc.

Super Searchers on Health & Medicine
The Online Secrets of Top Health & Medical Researchers

Susan M. Detwiler • Edited by Reva Basch

With human lives depending on them, skilled medical researchers rank among the best online searchers in the world. In *Super Searchers on Health & Medicine*, medical librarians, clinical researchers, health information specialists, and physicians explain how they combine traditional sources with the best of the Net to deliver just what the doctor ordered. If you use the Internet and online databases to answer important health and medical questions, these Super Searchers will help guide you around the perils and pitfalls to the best sites, sources, and techniques. As a reader bonus, "The Super Searchers Web Page" provides links to the most important Internet resources for health & medical researchers.

Softbound • ISBN 0-910965-44-7 • $24.95

Super Searchers in the News
The Online Secrets of Journalists & News Researchers

Paula J. Hane • Edited by Reva Basch

Professional news researchers are a breed apart. The behind-the-scenes heroes of network newsrooms and daily newspapers, they work under intense deadline pressure to meet the insatiable, ever-changing research needs of reporters, editors, and journalists. Here, for the first time, ten news researchers reveal their strategies for using the Internet and online services to get the scoop, check the facts, and nail the story. If you want to become a more effective online searcher and do fast, accurate research on a wide range of moving-target topics, don't miss *Super Searchers in the News*. As a bonus, a dedicated Web page links you to the most important Net-based information sources—Super Searcher tested and approved!

Softbound • ISBN 0-910965-45-5 • $24.95

Law of the Super Searchers
The Online Secrets of Top Legal Researchers

T.R. Halvorson • Edited by Reva Basch

In their own words, eight of the world's leading legal researchers explain how they use the Internet and online services to approach, analyze, and carry through a legal research project. In interviewing the experts, practicing attorney and online searcher T.R. Halvorson avoids the typical introductory approach to online research and focuses on topics critical to lawyers and legal research professionals: documenting the search, organizing a strategy, what to consider before logging on, efficient ways to build a search, and much more. *Law of the Super Searchers* offers fundamental strategies for legal researchers who need to take advantage of the wealth of information available online.

Softbound • ISBN 0-910965-34-X • $24.95

Super Searchers Do Business
The Online Secrets of Top Business Researchers

Mary Ellen Bates • Edited by Reva Basch

Super Searchers Do Business probes the minds of 11 leading researchers who use the Internet and online services to find critical business information. Through her in-depth interviews, Mary Ellen Bates—a business super searcher herself—gets the pros to reveal how they choose online sources, evaluate search results, and tackle the most challenging business research projects. Loaded with expert tips, techniques, and strategies, this is the first title in the exciting new "Super Searchers" series, edited by Reva Basch. If you do business research online, or plan to, let the Super Searchers be your guides.

Softbound• ISBN 0-910965-33-1 • $24.95

Millennium Intelligence
Understanding & Conducting Competitive Intelligence in the Digital Age

Edited by Jerry Miller

With contributions from the world's leading business intelligence practitioners, here is a tremendously informative and practical look at the CI process, how it is changing, and how it can be managed effectively in the Digital Age. Loaded with case studies, tips, and techniques, chapters include What Is Intelligence?; The Skills Needed to Execute Intelligence Effectively; Information Sources Used for Intelligence; The Legal and Ethical Aspects of Intelligence; Small Business Intelligence; Corporate Security and Intelligence; ... and much more!

Softbound • ISBN 0-910965-28-5 • $29.95

net.people
The Personalities and Passions Behind the Web Sites

Thomas E. Bleier and Eric C. Steinert

With the explosive growth of the Internet, people from all walks of life are bringing their dreams and schemes to life as Web sites. In *net.people*, authors Bleier and Steinert take you up close and personal with the creators of 35 of the world's most intriguing online ventures. For the first time, these entrepreneurs and visionaries share their personal stories and hard-won secrets of Webmastering. You'll learn how each of them launched a home page, increased site traffic, geared up for e-commerce, found financing, dealt with failure and success, built new relationships—and discovered that a Web site had changed their life forever.

Softbound • ISBN 0-910965-37-4 • $19.95

Internet Blue Pages, 2001-2002 Edition
The Guide to Federal Government Web Sites
Laurie Andriot

With over 1,800 Web addresses, this guide is designed to help you find any agency easily. Arranged in accordance with the US Government Manual, each entry includes the name of the agency, the Web address (URL), a brief description of the agency, and links to the agency's or subagency's home page. For helpful cross-referencing, an alphabetical agency listing and a comprehensive index for subject searching are also included. Regularly updated information and links are provided on the author's Web site.

Softbound • ISBN 0-910965-29-3 • $34.95

The Extreme Searcher's Guide To
Web Search Engines
A Handbook for the Serious Searcher
Randolph Hock

"Extreme searcher" Randolph (Ran) Hock—internationally respected Internet trainer and authority on Web search engines—offers advice designed to help you get immediate results. Ran not only shows you what's "under the hood" of the major search engines, but explains their relative strengths and weaknesses, reveals their many (and often overlooked) special features, and offers tips and techniques for searching the Web more efficiently and effectively than ever. Updates and links are provided at the author's Web site.

Softbound • ISBN 0-910965-26-9 • $24.95   Hardcover • ISBN 0-910965-38-2 • $34.95

Great Scouts!
CyberGuides for Subject Searching on the Web
Nora Paul and Margot Williams • Edited by Paula J. Hane

Great Scouts! is a cure for information overload. Authors Nora Paul (The Poynter Institute) and Margot Williams *(The Washington Post)* direct readers to the very best subject-specific, Web-based information resources. Thirty chapters cover specialized "CyberGuides" selected as the premier Internet sources of information on business, education, arts and entertainment, science and technology, health and medicine, politics and government, law, sports, and much more. With its expert advice and evaluations of information and link content, value, currency, stability, and usability, *Great Scouts!* takes you "beyond search engines"—and directly to the top sources of information for your topic. As a reader bonus, the authors are maintaining a Web page featuring updated links to all the sites covered in the book.

Softbound • ISBN 0-910965-27-7 • $24.95